HOW TO MAKE MONEY IN STOCKS

2022

THE BEST GUIDE TO STOCK MARKET INVESTING
FOR BEGINNERS

CONTENTS

INTRODUCTION

Many people do not realize it, but right now, we are undergoing a kind of economic revolution. It is a more subtle kind of revolution, less with parades and fanfare, but it is still radical nonetheless. This current economic revolution could completely change the way that people relate to money and finances.

When people talk about a "revolution," it is usually meant to signify some kind of large-scale changing of hands. A revolution defines a new era, a new epoch in history that operates on a different framework than previous eras. In today's financial world, the revolution we are seeing is the rise of self-guided investing.

Now I know what you are thinking: "What is this guy talking about? People have been investing forever." And this is true; investing itself is not new. However, what is new is that the average person now has all the tools and means to fully take control of their finances through investing. The normal person now has the option to invest and trade on the same terms with the big players.

In the past, here is how investing would work. You would have to make phone calls to buy and sell stock. You would call the brokerage firm, give the order to buy or sell, and then physical documents recording stock ownership would have to be shipped to your address. Before phones, investing mostly had to be done in person at a physical stock exchange. Needless to say, investing is much more accessible and streamlined nowadays.

In the past, the barriers to entry for stock trading made it primarily undertaken only by the upper echelons of society. You had to be wealthy enough to not only take work off to go to a stock exchange, but you also had to hire a brokerage firm and advisors to actually execute trades for you. Sure, there was the occasional average Joe or two who managed a modicum of success, but for the most part, these rich capitalists of yesteryear held the keys to the kingdom and kept everyone else out.

Nowadays, thanks to the internet, the stock game has completely changed. For the first time in history, everyday retail investors have the means and opportunity to compete in the stock market on their own terms. Online investing has caused a significant decentralization in how stock trading works and has opened up a huge space for everyday retail investors like yourself to take a piece of the pie. The stock market no longer needs to be entirely dominated by hedge funds and ultra-billionaires anymore; it's time for the regular people to enjoy the gains of investing.

Especially in today's economy, where wages have been stagnant, and jobs are harder than ever to come by, young people need a new way to navigate the world of finance. The bottom line is, Millennials can't keep doing the same thing that their Boomer and Gen-X parents did. The economy never really went back to "normal" after the Great Recession of 2008, and similarly, the economy will never go back to normal after the wave of political and economic instability that rocked the back half of the 2010s. It is time for Millennials to start taking their finances into their own hands, and modern stock trading is one way to do that.

Things have fundamentally changed, and a new world has opened up for investors. And it is my goal to show the average person that they do not have to do the same 9-5 grind anymore; that they can do something else and achieve the security and stability that their parents and grandparents were able to achieve.

My name is Fred Green, and I have over 25 years of experience helping my clients achieve their financial goals. I have worked for some of the largest brokerage firms in the country, so I understand how the largest players work and how the average person can compensate. I have helped countless people obtain financial wellness throughout my career and have the track record to back those claims up.

Most importantly, I understand how the economy is changing and how the average person can keep up and take advantage of these shifts. This book aims to educate a new generation of traders on everything they need to know to make their mark in the stock market and achieve financial independence. Throughout the course of this book, you will learn about:

- The fundamentals of investing
- How to buy and sell stock
- Different types of investments and asset classes
- How to understand share price, buying, and selling
- Technical measurements like P/E ratios and moving average
- Researching stocks and financial news
- How to analyze sectors and industries in the market
- Dollar-cost averaging and other simple trading strategies
- How markets and economics relate to one another
- How to build your passive wealth
- And more

By the end, you should walk away with a solid grasp of how you can open an investment account, pick investments, and manage your portfolio to minimize risk and maximize returns. You will also learn a thing or two about the broader theories of economics, finance, and how the two work together. Most importantly, you will have a solid grasp of how to invest in the modern era and what kinds of challenges and opportunities there might be in the modern economy.

So if you are interested in trading but don't really know where to start or have trouble keeping track of the bases, this book will provide everything you need to know. At the end of the day, there is only so much you can learn from reading a book. The real expertise and know-how come from actually doing. Just like with a sport, the more you practice trading, the more intuitive and second-nature the practice will come to you. You will be better able to "feel" out patterns in data and make smart investments using the broad base of knowledge that you have cultivated and refined through practice and experience.

So without any further ado, let's get to learning.

INTRO TO MARKETS

"To know values is to know the meaning of the market."

— CHARLES DOW

WHAT ARE MARKETS?

Many people consider the "market" to be the fundamental object of interest when it comes to investing. The term "market" is used to refer to all kinds of things, labor markets, housing markets, currency markets (even the dating market!), but across all these manifestations, markets share a critical unifying principle. Markets arise when individuals begin assigning exchange value to specific items. In other words, markets can be understood as complex systems that emerge out of the human tendency to give value to certain things.

Thus, markets ultimately are a place where people buy and sell things based on their perceived value. The stock market allows you to buy and sell assets. As the perceived value of your assets changes, the total value of your assets can increase or decrease. This all sounds theoretical and abstract, but the bottom line is that market forces are ultimately driven by people's preferences and subjective value judgments.

When people talk about "investing in the stock market," what they mean is that they want to buy stocks, wait for the value to increase, then sell them later to turn a profit. The entire mechanism of capital appreciation is what is behind how wealth grows in the stock market. According to capital appreciation rules, the value of something you own can change over time, depending on how desirable others perceive it.

All of this is to say that stock markets allow you to buy assets that can increase in value over time, thus generating more money than you started with. Humans' peculiar tendency is to change their value judgments depending on conditions that explain why stocks can vary in value daily.

Many books talk about stocks and investing, but rarely do they ever answer the fundamental question of *why* investing works the way that it does. Once you realize that markets are ultimately an expression of peoples' value judgments, it makes sense that market conditions can change depending on how people's subjective value judgments change.

This realization will help you understand why stock prices may change in the way they do as they depend on subjective human factors. It will also help you better anticipate future changes in stock prices. Also, understanding how the stock market depends on people's attitudes and preferences will keep your own attitudes and preferences in check, so you do not get too emotional and make a rash decision.

HOW TO INVEST IN THE STOCK MARKET

The primary question is: How do I invest in the stock market? Fortunately, it is effortless to do so.

To invest in the stock market, you need 2 things: A brokerage firm and capital.

A brokerage firm is an entity that facilitates trades on the market. Brokers provide a place where you can make trades and store your money, which significantly streamlines the investment process. In exchange, a broker might take a small percentage fee of assets or transactions. You can open a *brokerage account,* which is an account through the broker that you use to make investments.

Strictly speaking, you do not *need* to trade through a broker. Many companies have direct stock purchasing plans, so you can circumvent buying through a broker. However, for the vast majority of individual and institutional investors, going through a broker will be the better choice, hands down. Brokers not only provide a wide selection of stocks to buy, but they will also keep documents of your transactions, capital gains, etc.; all things you will need for taxes and legal purposes. Broker platforms also usually have research articles and statistical analysis tools.

Second, investors need capital, which is a fancy word for "money." It makes sense: if you want to invest, you need money to invest. You can't buy shares unless you already have some cash lying around. The trick here is that you do not need a ton of money to get started investing. In the past, when there were more barriers to entry, investing required a larger initial sum. However, many modern brokerages allow you to begin investing with as little as $1.

Once you find those two things, you can open a brokerage account and start picking stocks to buy. Here's how.

HOW TO OPEN AN ACCOUNT

If you decide to trade through a broker, the very first thing you need to do is open a brokerage account. Online brokerages are the most efficient way to trade in the modern era, so this guide will be based on the assumption that you have chosen an online brokerage. Nowadays, most online brokers do not charge commission for regular day trades and do not have minimum deposits to get started investing. Here is a quick list of some of the most popular no-fee online brokers at the moment:

- Robinhood
- TD Ameritrade
- Charles Schwab
- Fidelity
- M1 Finance
- Vanguard
- Betterment

These are just a handful, but there are literally hundreds more to pick. Some platforms might be oriented towards basic stock trading, while others might have a niche focus, like commodities or foreign currencies.

Whichever platform you pick, make sure that it does not charge fees for regular trades and has lower than 0.50% annual account fees. Eliminating fees on traditional transactions will save you a ton of money in the long run. Most brokers will charge an account or management fee, usually a percentage of the total amount of money you have invested through the platform. However, some brokers will not charge an account fee.

Once you pick a broker, you need to make an account. The exact details will differ from broker to broker, but you will likely have to give at least your name, a valid email address, social security number, some kind of proof of ID, and a bank account number to fund your account. You will also be asked a short questionnaire on your risk tolerance and investment preferences on many brokerages. These kinds of questionnaires are meant to help the platform recommend various investments that fit your preferences.

Once your account has been created, verified, and funded, you can then start buying stocks.

Traditional Broker vs. Robo Advisor

There are two ways you can go about picking and choosing investments. First, you can go the traditional brokerage route and manually create a **portfolio**. A portfolio is a term for your collection of investments. This standard model of investing gives you more or less complete control over what your portfolio looks like, what its allocations are, and whether you want to add or remove shares. Most online brokerages nowadays operate on this traditional model.

However, there is now the choice of a Robo advisor. A Robo advisor is an automated service that uses algorithms to automatically buy and sell assets to keep your portfolio within predefined metrics. Robo advisors automate the process, so you don't have to manually monitor your portfolio. Most Robo advisors allow you to choose between 5-12 predefined stock portfolios that the algorithm will take care of for you. Robo advisors are a very streamlined way to invest, but you will not be able to customize the contents of the portfolio that you choose most of the time. So, if you select a Robo advisor, the trade-off will be portfolio flexibility.

That being said, there are many reasons to choose a Robo advisor. First of all, since they essentially eliminate the human element of investing, they have lower fees than a traditional brokerage. Most Robo advisor firms have annual fees as low as 0.25%, potentially lower. That means that less of your hard-earned money will go to fees.

Robo advisors also are good for passive investing. If you do not have the time or effort to devote to actively managing your portfolios, then a Robo advisor can be an excellent way to pick up the slack so you can focus on other things. Some people are not interested in learning all about stocks, so they are content to let intelligent robots handle all the nitty-gritty details for them.

Lastly, Robo advisors have been shown to be profitable. Pretty much every modern Robo advisory service uses algorithms based on cutting-edge economics and finance. More specifically, modern Robo advisors are built around Nobel Laureate Harry Markowitz's Modern Portfolio Theory (MPT).

Later in this book, we will cover Modern Portfolio Theory and talk about why it is a vital paradigm shift for investing. Suffice to say, for now, Robo advisors have been built with the best economic science in mind so that they can compete with traditional brokerages in most cases.

HOW TO BUY STOCK

Do Research

Now that you have your account set up and funded, it's time to actually buy some stocks. First, you will need to do some research. It helps to start by looking at big companies that you are already familiar with through your experiences as a consumer. At first, you do not need to worry about all the fancy technical jargon and numbers. Just ask yourself the simple question: *What company would I like to own part of?* Investing is a lot more meaningful when you put your money in companies you actually like than just those you think stock prices will go up.

Once you identify a few companies, start looking for their annual reports. Most of the time, you can find these documents by Googling "[Company name] annual reports." Publicly traded companies are required by law to give investors detailed records of fiscal performance so that you can find these materials relatively easily. Management has to send quarterly updates to shareholders, so you should be able to find releases from within the past few months.

Your brokerage should also have supplementary data like share price history, SEC filings, conference call transcripts, updates, and news, in addition to technical tools for analysis. You can search for the company on your platform with the ticker name to find its stock for purchase.

Determine How Many Shares to Buy

Now you need to determine how many shares you should buy. We highly recommend just starting with one or two shares in the company you have chosen. That will give you enough exposure to get a feel for how share price changes over time while also not exposing you to very much risk. You can always add more to your portfolio as time goes on, but that first stock purchase should be minimal and modest.

Fractional Shares

Many brokers also offer "fractional shares," so you can buy just a portion of stock instead of the whole thing. Fractional shares are a way that investors without much capital can still invest in larger companies that might have a very high share price, such as Amazon or Google. Robinhood and Charles Schwab are two no-fee brokers that allow fractional share trading. Cash app and even Venmo are starting to get in the mix by offering fractional shares to purchase stocks. The benefit of fractional shares is that you can have a properly diversified portfolio even with minimal amounts of capital.

Make an Order

The next step is to select your order type. Many different order types can get complex, but the only two orders that you need to know right now are a **market order** and a **limit order.**

A market order is simply a request to buy or sell a particular stock right now at the current best price. A limit order is a request to buy or sell a stock when it hits a specific price or lower/higher. There are dozens of other order types, but many successful investors go their entire careers with just making these two types of orders.

When you make a market order, you are asking to buy or sell the stock immediately at whatever price is current. Most of the time, market orders will go through very quickly unless you buy a massive volume of shares or unusually high trading activity. Share prices change continuously throughout the day, so don't be surprised if the price you pay is not the exact price that was on the screen just a few seconds before you confirm the trade.

Limit orders are designed so you can wait until share prices hit a particular mark before buying or selling. For example, say you want stock XYZ but it is trading for $100 and you think that is too expensive. You can put in a limit order to wait and execute a trade when XYZ's share price drop to $90. Limit orders can ensure that you get a fair share price, but it may not be filled if the share price doesn't hit the limit.

Own Your Stocks

Once the market or limit order is cleared, you will then be the proud new owner of your first shiny stock; congratulations! But, you are only just getting started. That first stock can serve as the seed for your portfolio as you add to it over time. In fact, many portfolios are built around a core group of stable securities with flexibility in other allocations. Once you start buying stock, the key is to optimize your portfolio performance by finding the right mix between risk and return. We will cover the concepts more in-depth in a later chapter.

COMMON MISTAKES BEGINNER INVESTORS MAKE

When you are just starting, you will definitely make some mistakes. This is entirely normal. It would be impossible to find a trader that hasn't messed up or made a bad call in the past. That being said, you should try to avoid any mistakes as much as possible. Here are some common pitfalls that several beginner investors fall into:

Underdiversification

Probably the single biggest pitfall new inventors fall into is that they do not property diversify their portfolios. When we say that a portfolio is diversified, we mean that it has stocks and assets that are spread out over several companies, industries, and sectors. Diversification makes sure that your portfolio is insulated from losses if one of your investments goes south.

Here is a simple example showing why diversification is essential. Say you dump all of your money in stock from one company. The company stock then tanks, and you lose all your money. Now, if you have spread your investments over multiple assets, then the others can pick up the slack if another fails. Have you ever heard the phrase: "Don't put all your eggs in one basket"? The same principle is behind diversification. An underdiversified portfolio is probably the biggest vulnerability a portfolio can have.

Panic Buying/Selling

Another common pitfall that new investors fall into is panic buying and selling. When prices fluctuate wildly up and down, investors might panic and sell off any losing investments to stymie their losses. However, this rapid panic buying can lead to a chain reaction that causes share prices to fall even more. Even worse, many people sell off their assets and then no longer own the stock when it inevitably corrects. The person who just panicked and sold their assets is out of luck.

It can be very frustrating and anxiety-inducing when you see that the value of your investments has dropped by 10% in a single day, but you need to resist the instinctual urge to drop any assets that might have taken a loss. In almost every case, when there is a big jump in share price, there will be a period where share price stabilizes and equalizes. Patterns of panic buying and selling are believed to be the primary mechanisms behind the dot-com bubble burst in 2001 and the housing crisis of 2008.

Familiarity Bias

Familiarity bias refers to the tendency of a person to prefer certain investment decisions in their own companies, sectors, regions, states, or countries. Specific examples of familiarity bias might include a person's preference to support companies in their geographic area over others or domestic over international companies. In and of itself, investing in things that you are familiar with is not bad. It only becomes a losing strategy when familiarity beats out rational analysis.

For example, studies have shown that employees often want to invest in employer stock, even though they already have a stake in company performance without investing. If an employee invests all of their money in the company they work for, and the company fails, the investor could compound their losses. This is what happened to several Enron and Fannie Mae employees, two companies that went under after committing fraud.

Noise Trading

When you are just starting with trading, it can be hard to differentiate realistic signals of market movements from random fluctuations. The term "noise" refers to aberrations and short-term volatility that does not indicate a larger trend. So-called "noise-traders" often trade on overhyped news reports, small movements that don't display actual movement or overreact to good or bad news.

As you might expect, noise trading is very easy to fall into if you are too excited or earnest to start investing. You might notice a temporary fluctuation and extrapolate to more extensive non-existent trends. Or maybe you read an article about a new product company X is launching and greatly overestimate how much that news will cause share prices to move.

WHAT MAKES A GOOD INVESTOR?

The term "good investor" is a bit subjective. The meaning of the term can differ depending on what your investing goals are. A good long-term investor might act differently than a good day trader or swing trader.

That being said, here are some general behaviors that most good investors will demonstrate.

- **Your portfolio is adequately diversified.** Diversification is a good sign of an investor that is in tune with market movements. A diverse portfolio includes a diverse array of companies and asset types such as shares, bonds, ETFs, etc.
- **You don't buy or sell with emotion.** Being a good investor involves creating a plan and sticking to it, whether or not there is market volatility.
- **You save an appreciable part of your income.** Common wisdom holds that you should save at least 20% of your income. In reality, most people manage around 10%-15%, which is still good. If you are investing at least 10% of your monthly income, you are smart with building your wealth.
- **You are smart with taxation.** There are several tricks and things you can do to reduce your overall taxable burden. Things like tax-loss harvesting or taking advantage of tax-deferred investment accounts are all ways to lower your overall taxable burden and keep more of your hard-earned money.
- **You focus on the fundamentals of investments.** Good investors do not just make investments based on price movements. This kind of momentum investing is extremely risky and does not generate maximal returns. A good investor instead focuses on fundamental value-generating aspects of a company like revenue, performance, reputation, and product selection. If you can dig into an investment and find more value that is not accounted for in the share price, you might be a good investor.

DEFINING STOCKS

We have already used the term "stocks" and "stock" market many times already, so you might be wondering; *Just what, exactly, is a stock?*

So in this chapter, we will cover the basics of stocks, how they work, features and important metrics or stocks, and how stocks can be used to build a killer investment portfolio that maximizes gains while minimizing risks.

WHAT ARE STOCKS?

Stocks, also known as *equities*, are the thing that makes investing go round in the first place. In simple terms, a stock represents a piece of ownership in a business or corporation. Someone who owns stock is a part-owner of a company. The more stock a person owns, the larger a chunk of a company they own. Individual units of stocks are called **shares.** (Note: "Stock" or "stocks" can both be used as a plural noun).

Ok, but what's so essential about ownership, you ask? Stock entitles the owner to a portion of the company's assets and profits. That means that the value of individual shares is directly correlated with the value of a particular business. Stocks are bought and sold on stock exchanges, but companies also perform private sales directly to investors. Investors who own shares in a company are called "shareholders."

The real amazing thing about stocks is that their value can increase over time, and you do not have to do a single thing. If you buy shares in a company, and the company does well, the value of your individual shares will increase. So, for example, say you buy 100 shares for $1 each. Then, say the price of each individual share rises to $2 per share. Now those shares are collectively worth $200. You just gained $100, and you didn't have to lift a finger!

WHY DO COMPANIES SELL STOCK?

Corporations and large companies need a lot of money to fund their projects. The problem is that the company's founders will rarely have the necessary liquid startup capital just lying around. So, companies will sell shares to individual investors to raise money for projects and expansion. Companies offer a portion of ownership and profits in exchange for buying stock to incentivize investors.

Stocks represent a portion of ownership in a company. The more stocks an individual owns, the larger their portion of ownership over a company is. An investor's ownership depends on the number of shares they have compared to the total number of shares outstanding. For example, if a company has 10,000 total outstanding shares, and one person owns 2,000 of them, then that person has a 20% stake in the company.

It is essential to understand that stock ownership is different from owning a corporation and all of its assets. Company property is legally distinct from the shareholders' property to minimize the liability of both parties. Corporations are legally treated like persons, which means that they can own their assets. So, if a corporation goes bankrupt, the company might have to sell off its assets (e.g., desks, equipment, buildings, etc.), but creditors cannot come after shareholders' personal assets. Shareholders are not even forced to sell their shares if a company goes bankrupt, although their shares are likely to decrease in price drastically.

This difference between corporate ownership and shareholder ownership is sometimes called "separation of ownership and control." This principle basically means that shareholders cannot do whatever they want with a company's assets, like walk into an office and take a chair home. Stocks entitle you to a portion of a company's profits, but these profits are often reinvested to scale and grow operations. These profits are still reflected in the share price of the stock, however.

CLASSES OF STOCKS

There are two major classes of stocks that are sold on exchanges: **common stocks** and **preferred stocks.**

Common stocks are the most numerous kinds of stock, and most shareholders have common stock. Common stock typically gives holders the right to vote on important issues affecting company leadership and control. Common stock may also entitle the owner to **dividends.** Dividends are a portion of earnings that are paid directly to shareholders. If someone decides to sell their shares, these entitlements pass to the new shareholder. Common stock shares are often called "Class-A" shares.

The more common stock a person has, the more voting rights they have. Shareholders are the ones who appoint the company's board of directors. The goal of the board of directors is to increase the company's value for shareholders. It is they who are responsible for appointing CEOs, CTOs, and other management positions in the company.

So, if an entity controls the majority of most common stock, they effectively control the company by controlling the board of directors. This happens when one company acquires another; one company buys up all the shares of another company.

The other major kind of stock is preferred stock. Preferred stockholders do not typically have voting rights in the company, but they are entitled to a more significant percentage of company assets and earnings. Preferred stockholders receive priority when it comes to distributing dividends and are also first in line if the company goes bankrupt and is liquidated. Preferred stock shares are often called "Class-B" shares.

Other Ways to Categorize Stocks

Common stock and preferred stock are the two major kinds of shares, but shares can also be categorized in many other ways. For example, stocks can be categorized by the total value of all outstanding shares. Companies with a total outstanding share value of less than $2 billion are considered *small-cap* stocks, while shares from companies worth more than $10 billion are called *large-cap* stocks. Shares from companies with a total value between $2 billion and $10 billion are called *mid-cap* stocks.

You can also categorize stocks based on the kind of industry or sector that the company is in, such as:

- **Health care.** Drug companies, hospitals, medical tech, health insurance, and health care providers.
- **Basic materials.** Natural resource extraction (e.g., coal, oil, natural gas)
- **Industrial.** Companies that manufacture goods
- **Service.** Companies that provide products and services to consumers
- **Tech.** Computers, communications, software, etc.
- **Financial.** Banks, real estate, insurance companies, etc.
- **Retail.** Companies that provide goods to buy at retail for consumers (e.g., Target, Wal-Mart)
- **Utilities.** Companies that provide electricity, gas, water, sewage, and other necessities (might include broadband companies and internet providers)

You can also divide stocks based on their expected behavior. *Growth stocks* are stocks that investors think will grow very rapidly. Tech and healthcare companies are often considered growth stocks by investors because they tend to grow quickly but tend not to pay out dividends. *Value stocks* are stocks that pay decent dividends. Utility stocks are often considered value stocks. *Blue-chip stocks* refer to shares of large, well-known companies that may not grow quickly but are reliable and stable.

There are essentially limitless ways to categorize stocks, depending on what aspects you are interested in.

BUYING AND SELLING STOCKS

As stated previously, companies sell shares to raise capital to fund projects and expansion. The first time a company sells shares to investors is called the company's **initial public offering** (IPO).

When created, buying shares directly from companies is called a *primary market*, while the secondary market is where investors trade shares. Investment banks determine the value that shares sell for during an IPO. Companies hire investment banks to assess their value and assign a proper share price for an IPO.

In the secondary market, the share price is determined by supply and demand. The more people sell a particular stock, the less desirable it is perceived to be, and the share price will drop. Conversely, as more people buy shares in a company, it is perceived as more valuable, and the share price will rise.

The total amount of shares that change hands in a given period is called the *trading volume*. Trading volumes can be defined on a daily, monthly, or yearly basis. Shares with high trading volumes are usually subject to more significant price fluctuations than shares with low trading volumes.

Most of the time, investor buying and selling behavior is determined by their expectations for company performance. If investors expect earnings and revenue to be high, then they will bid up the share price with one another.

When a person buys shares for one price, then the shares increase in value; that is called a gain. Gains can be *realized* or *unrealized*. Realized gains are gains that are made from actually selling stocks and receiving liquid cash. Unrealized gains (also called "paper gains") are gains that have not been realized yet. When shares are sold and a gain goes from unrealized to realized, we say that the gain has been *actualized*. It's important to understand that realized gains and unrealized gains are treated differently for tax purposes. Realizing a gain is a taxable event (because you actually have the money) but unrealized gains are not taxable. Taxes paid on realized gains are called *capital gains taxes*.

Typically, investors hold onto unrealized gains because they believe that the investment will continue to grow. The longer an investor holds on to an unrealized gain, the lower capital gains tax they will have to pay when they realize that gain. Gains made after holding on to a stock for longer than one year are called *long-term gains* and are taxed at a lower capital gains rate. Investors might also hold off on realizing gains until the following year to decrease their overall tax burden for the current year.

(**Note:** Money received from capital gains is legally considered distinct from income, like the money you get from your job or dividends/interest.)

STOCK TICKER SYMBOLS

Each stock has a unique symbol or series of letters that is used to identify it on an exchange. The specific stock symbol depends on the specific exchange where the stock is listed. This symbol is also sometimes called a stock **ticker**. For example, the ticker symbol for Apple on the NASDAQ is AAPL.

You can think of ticker symbols as a nickname to search for stocks on an exchange. Exchanges started using ticker symbols during the 1800s as the number of traded companies rapidly began to expand. Traders soon realized it was too difficult to keep track of every company's full names, so they agreed to assign every company a unique code of letters. These unique symbols help differentiate shares from companies that might have similar names. For example, on the NYSE, CIT Group and Citigroup have different ticker symbols CIT and C, respectively.

Ticker symbols also identify when a company has different classes of share, such as common and preferred. For example, if the shares are preferred, then the ticker symbol might have the letters PR before the company symbol. Alphabet Inc., the parent company of Google, has two classes of shares designated GOOGL and GOOG. GOOGL shares come with voting rights, while GOOG shares do not.

Ticker symbols may have extra letters to indicate certain features of the shares or status of the company. On the NASDAQ, the letter 'W' is added to the ticker symbols of companies that are delinquent. Companies that are undergoing bankruptcy proceedings are often designated with a 'Q.'Non-US companies trading on US exchanges typically have a 'Y' in the ticker symbol. Here is a list of the different ticker modifiers used on the NASDAQ.

- A: Class A shares
- B: Class B shares
- C: Issuer Qualification Exception - lacks some exchange requirements but has an exception and can be listed.
- D: New issue of existing stock
- E: Is delinquent due to missing one or more SEC required filings

(alternate symbol: LF)

- F: Foreign issue
- G: First convertible bond
- H: Second convertible bond
- I: Third convertible bond
- J: Voting shares
- K: Non-voting shares
- L: Miscellaneous
- M: Fourth-class preferred shares
- N: Third-class preferred shares
- O: Second-class preferred shares
- P: First-class preferred shares
- Q: Currently undergoing bankruptcy proceedings
- R: Rights
- S: Shares of beneficial interest
- T: Warrants or with rights
- U: Units
- V: Shares that are going through some announced corporate action plan such as a stock split or reverse split
- W: Warrants
- X: Mutual Funds
- Y: American Depository Receipt (ADR)
- Z: Miscellaneous (same meaning as symbol L)
- OB: Over-the-counter bulletin board
- PK: Pink sheets
- SC: Small-cap stocks
- NM: National Market

BID-ASK SPREAD

The bid-ask spread is one of the most important fundamental ideas that all investors need to know. The bid-ask spread is crucial because it partially determines the share price on an exchange. The *bid price* refers to the maximum amount the buyer is willing to pay for a particular share. The *ask price* is the minimum that the seller is willing to sell the share for. The difference between the bid price and ask price is called the *spread*. For example, if the bid price for a share is $10.50 and the ask price is $10.40, then the spread is $0.10.

The bid-ask spread is important because it tells you how liquid a particular share is. The smaller the spread is, the more liquid the shares are. The more liquid some shares are, the easier it is to convert those shares into cash. If the spread is very large, then there is a bigger mismatch between how much people want to buy the share for and how much people want to sell the shares for. As a result, fewer shares are sold, as it's harder for buyers and sellers to agree on a transaction.

In general, you want to find securities that have a relatively narrow bid-ask spread. The narrower this spread, the easier it will be to trade those securities. Shares that have high liquidity typically experience growth because a large volume is constantly trading hands every day.

Bid-ask spreads are determined by the actual buying and selling behavior of investors. If demand is higher than the supply, then the share price will rise. Conversely, if demand is lower than the supply, the share price will decrease. Shares that have a high trading volume tend to have narrow bid-ask spreads while shares that have a low trading volume tend to have wider bid-ask spreads.

Here is an example illustrating how bid-ask spreads work in markets. Say that Company A wants to buy 100 shares of stock XYZ at $10 a share and Company B is willing to sell 100 shares at $10.10 a share. In this case, the spread would be $10.10-$10.00 = $0.10.

An investor looking at these numbers then knows that they could sell 100 shares of XYZ to Company A for $10 a share, or they could buy 100 shares of XYZ from Company B for $10.10 a share.

Some larger firms, called *market makers, will* often set bid-ask spreads to buy and sell stock. In this case, the bid-ask spread is important because it represents the profit the firm gets. If you fill a market order to buy or sell from the firm, you will receive either the highest or lowest price.

COST BASIS

Another basic feature of stocks that is important to understand is the cost basis. The cost basis refers to the original price paid for an investment. The cost basis is important because it determines the total amount of capital gains tax you pay on your investments. Calculating the cost basis of a particular investment can help you determine if it will be profitable or not. When gains are realized, the difference between the cost basis and selling price determines how much in taxes you will have to pay.

At a very base level, you can think of the cost basis as the total amount you paid for an investment, plus any fees or commissions. You can express the cost basis in total dollar amounts or per share. The total amount of capital gains that will be taxed is calculated as the difference between the cost basis and the sale price.

Here is a simple example of how this works. Say you buy 1,000 shares for $1 each, to a total of $1,000. Your cost basis in this example would be $1,000. Next, imagine the share price rises from $1 to $1.50, so your investment is now worth $1,500, and you sell those shares. The $500 difference between the cost basis and sale price is a taxable gain and will be subject to capital gains taxes.

It is very important to update your cost basis if you reinvest any dividends or other types of income generated from stocks. Doing so can ultimately lower the total amount of capital gains taxes you will have to pay, and your investment will be overall more profitable. Here is how:

Say you buy those $1,000 worth of shares and over a year those shares generate $200 in dividends that you reinvest to buy more shares. Your new cost basis would then be $1,200. Thus, any future capital gains will be calculated based on that updated cost basis. So if your investment increased in value to $1,500, then the only taxable gain would be the $300 difference. If you neglect to update your cost basis for investments, you can have a higher tax liability on capital gains than would generally be the case.

Investors make cost basis comparisons to determine which investments will be more profitable in the long run.

P/E RATIOS AND OTHER IMPORTANT STOCK ELEMENTS

Now that we have a working definition of stocks, we can dig more into the nitty-gritty of how specific stocks are analyzed and how you can find good investments. Specifically, in this chapter, we will take a look at the concepts of:

- P/E ratios
- Earnings per share
- Stock split/Reverse split
- Stock Tables
- Financial News

P/E RATIOS AND WHY THEY MATTER

The term price-to-earnings ratio (P/E ratio) is a measure of the price per individual share compared to the total earnings that the company makes. The P/E ratio is a measure that tells you how stocks are valued in the market, and whether they are overvalued or undervalued. The share price tells you how in demand a particular stock is, but the P/E ratio tells you whether the stock price is overvalued or undervalued compared to potential company earnings.

One of the key principles of value investing is to find companies that are trading at a relatively low price-to-earnings ratio. Stocks with a lower price per earnings ratio are more likely to be considered undervalued by investors and could be an excellent choice to add to your portfolio. Conversely, stocks that have a high P/E ratio might be considered overvalued and may not be as efficient as an investment for your portfolio compared to competitor stocks.

How to Calculate P/E Ratios

You can calculate the P/E ratio of a particular share by dividing the share price by the stocks total earnings:

$$\text{P/E Ratio} = \frac{Market\ value\ per\ share}{Earnings\ per\ share}$$

For example, if a company XYZ is selling at $50 a share, and each share can generate $5 in annual earnings, then the P/E ratio is 10 (50/5). You can interpret this number as saying that it would take 10 years for the $50 share to accumulate earnings equal to the initial cost of the investment.

According to this logic, you can see why lower P/E ratios are often a good choice for investors. Shares that have low P/E ratios maximize the buying power of your capital. The lower the P/E ratio, the less time it would take for the share to accumulate the value of the initial investment in earnings.

Take our previous example of company XYZ at $50 a share but instead let's say the earnings per share are $10 per year. In this case, the P/E ratio would be 5 (50/10). That means it would only take 5 years for the share to generate the initial cost of investment.

P/E ratios can be calculated for individual shares and they can also be applied to entire stock indexes and exchanges. P/E ratios can also be applied over different time frames, including weeks, months, and years.

It is important to realize that P/E ratios themselves will not tell you whether an investment is "good" or "bad." It is just one tool to get information about a stock. It needs to be contextualized upon other information about the stock and the company. However, P/E ratios are a very important part of stock analysis and need to be understood, especially if you are a value investor.

Types of P/E Ratios

The basic mathematics behind the P/E ratio is simple, but there are some variations on how you can calculate it. The simplest way is to calculate it using the current share price, but different calculation variations are useful for making predictions over different time frames. There are two major kinds of P/E ratios that beginner investors should be very familiar with: **trailing ratios** and **forward ratios**.

Trailing Ratios

One of the most common earnings measurements to use is the company's earnings over the past 12 calendar months. This "trailing" P/E ratio is often used in the evaluation of companies because it factors in historical data about actual company performance. P/E ratios can be calculated with TTM (trailing twelve months) Earnings by dividing the current stock price over the past 12 months of earnings per share. When people talk about the generic "P/E ratio" of a stock, they are most often referring to the TTM Earnings measurement.

This particular measurement is considered useful because it is based on historical performance over the past year. All other things being equal, it is assumed that a company's past earnings are a relatively good indicator of future earnings. But this connection is not absolute. Past earnings do not necessarily predict future earnings, so be careful relying solely on TTM Earnings To determine stock valuation.

Forward Ratios

Analysts will also sometimes make predictions about future earnings to calculate P/E ratios. These kinds of "forward earnings" do not rely on historical data but are instead based on projected performance in the following year. This means that P/E ratios calculated with predicted earnings can be misleading if actual company performance does not match up to expectations.

Say, for example, that company XYZ is currently trading at $50 a share and $5 in earnings per share. Analysts estimate that over the next year company earnings will grow by 10%. The current P/E ratio would be 50/5 = 10, but the forward P/E would be 50/(5x1.10) = 9.1. In this case, the forward P/E ratio is lower than the current P/E ratio because the calculation is factoring in the predicted increase in earnings over the next year.

Forward P/E ratios are used to understand differences in the relative value of companies that differ in share price. In the abstract, any amount of earnings at company A are worth exactly the same at company B. So, theoretically, the share prices of the two should be the same. However, companies with identical P/E ratios rarely ever actually trade at the same price.

If one company is trading at a higher share price than another, then evidence shows that the market values that company's earnings more somehow. One way to interpret this difference is that the higher valued company has higher projected earnings due to superior management, better products, or some other reason.

Other Kinds of P/E Ratios

There are many other ways to calculate P/E ratios, depending on which data points are relevant for your purposes and analysis. For example, one kind of "unorthodox" P/E ratio is the Shiller P/E ratio, which is calculated by dividing the current share price over the average earnings per share over the past 10 years when adjusted for inflation. The Shiller ratio is often used to calculate the P/E ratio of entire indexes and exchanges over extended periods of time. The Shiller P/E ratio of the S&P 500 index is just over 30, as of 2021.

P/E RATIOS: GROWTH AND VALUE STOCKS

One of the most common uses of the P/E ratio is to tell whether stocks are overvalued or undervalued. Stocks with a high P/E ratio are more expensive relative to earnings and stocks with lower P/E ratios are less expensive relative to earnings.

Through P/E ratios, stocks can be classified as "growth" and "value" stocks, two significant kinds of stocks that all investors need to know about.

Growth Stocks

Growth stocks are stocks that are expected to grow at rates significantly higher than the average market growth. Companies that issue growth stocks typically reinvest earnings into the company, so the stock continues to grow rapidly. This is one reason why growth stocks do not typically pay dividends: all of those earnings are put back into company growth. Investors are interested in growth stocks primarily because of the capital gains they expect those stocks to generate.

Growth stocks typically trade at a high P/E ratio, which is how you can identify them. The trick with growth stocks is that they may not be a good deal at the moment, but they are expected to grow quickly in the future and generate a large return on investment. Because the value of a growth stock is dependent on its projected future performance, it can be risky to invest in nothing but growth stocks. However, growth stocks are an integral part of any properly diversified portfolio.

Growth stocks can be found in every industry, but they tend to share some key features. Growth stocks are generally from companies that provide unique products and services to people. Tech stocks are commonly considered growth stocks because those companies reinvest profits to develop more tech and expand operations. Pharmaceutical stocks are also often considered growth stocks for the same reason: the company puts all the profits back into R&D (Research and Development).

Since growth stocks trade at high P/E ratios, they can look like they are too expensive. However, they can still be a good choice because earnings growth is expected to significantly boost share price in the near future.

Value Stocks

On the other end of the spectrum from growth stocks are value stocks. Value stocks are shares that are trading at a lower price relative to total company earnings. The lower P/E ratio of value stocks is usually interpreted as meaning the stock is undervalued and that it would be a good investment for a long-term horizon. Value investors look for value stocks to take advantage of inefficiencies in the market if the pricing of a stock does not match the company's actual performance.

Typically, good candidates for value stocks have low P/E ratios and high dividend yields. These kinds of stocks generate a lot of value relative to the overall share price. They also might have a lower share price than other similarly sized competitor companies despite having similar fundamental metrics.

One way to think of what value investing is doing is highlighting the difference between the market value of a stock (i.e., share price) and the so-called *intrinsic value* of a stock. The intrinsic value of a stock is determined by several factors, including the company's performance, earnings, book value, public reputation, management, and labor force. The market value of a security may not accurately reflect the intrinsic value of a stock. Stocks that have a high intrinsic value relative to share value are good candidates for value stocks.

Value stocks are often considered riskier investments than growth stocks because markets tend to view value stocks with a bit of skepticism. There is no guarantee that value stocks will exit from their undervalued position, so you are taking a risk that the company will improve its performance in the long run. Given the higher risks, value investing can generate high returns.

Sectors that are commonly considered to have value stocks include finance, energy/utilities, and basic materials companies. These companies tend to have high cash flows and trade on the market at a significant discount relative to their total earnings. It is tricky to identify value stocks because gauging intrinsic value is a highly subjective process. But some of the wealthiest investors in the world such as Warren Buffett have built their fortunes on a strategy of value investing.

STOCK SPLITS & REVERSE SPLITS

Say you have a $20 bill and someone offers you two $10s in exchange for it. Most people might be ambivalent about the trade as they end up with the same amount of money as they had previously. Something similar can happen in the stock world—**stock splits**. Unlike our example with dollar bills, stock splits can be a highly lucrative opportunity for investors.

A stock split is a type of corporate action in which a company increases the total number of outstanding shares by dividing ("splitting") shares into multiple ones. The result of a stock split is that there is a great number of total outstanding shares, but the individual price of each share is less. Since stock splits do not add any capital, they do not change the total *market capitalization* of the company—the total dollar amount of all outstanding shares added together.

For example, with a 2-to-1 stock split, every shareholder will get 2 shares for every share they currently have, but the price of each share will be reduced by half. Similarly, with a 3-to-1 stock split, shareholders will get 3 shares for every 1 share they currently have, but individual share price will be reduced by a factor of 3. Similar to the case with the dollar bills, the total value of your investment stays the same.

One reason for stock splits is to incentivize people to buy more shares. When share prices get too high, some investors might be discouraged from buying. Stock splits effectively increase the total number of shares so more people can buy them for a cheaper price. Stocks that have very high share prices may have large bid-ask spreads, and thus a lower trading volume. The result is that stock splits can significantly increase the liquidity of shares by increasing the overall trading volume.

Companies may also perform **reverse stock splits**. With a reverse stock split, the total number of outstanding shares is *decreased* by combining existing shares into single units. Similar to a stock split, a reverse stock split does not change the market capitalization for the company, but it does increase the individual share price. For example, with a 1-to-5 split, every 5 shares an investor has is combined to make 1 share. The total number of shares shrinks by 5x, but the individual share price increases by 5x.

The reasons for a reverse stock split are largely the same as a regular stock split. If the share price is too low, then this discourages trading. Reducing the total number of shares but increasing their individual values is meant to boost the appearance of the stock and increase trading volume. Reverse stock splits can also keep stock from being delisted from an exchange for trading at too low a share price. For instance, the NASDAQ will not list stock trading at less than $1 per share.

However, reverse stock splits are often a result of a company recently losing substantial value. As such, reverse stock splits have a somewhat negative connotation in the financial world.

How Do Stock Splits Affect Your Equity?

In a strict mathematical sense, stock splits should have no real effect on the value of a stock as the ratio of share price to total outstanding shares remains the same. However, humans are not purely mathematical creatures and we do all kinds of irrational things. When a company does a stock split, there might be a small price surge in share price because the split might drum up interest in shares. If you have a lot of shares, you can profit a tidy sum on any short-term price increases right after a split.

As a real-world example, Apple shares were trading for over $600 back in 2013. This share price was too high for most retail investors. Apple performed a 7-to-1 stock split which reduced the share price to $92. The next day, the share price rose by $3 due to increased interest and trading. If you had owned 1,000 shares before the split, then you would have owned 7,000 shares after the split and made a tidy profit of $3 x 7000 = $21,000 after the share price rose. Not too shabby of a profit all things considered.

Conversely, a reverse stock split can have the opposite effect. Reverse stock splits are usually a sign of low investor confidence, resulting in the share price falling. Reverse stock splits were very popular shortly following the dot-com bubble burst as thousands of companies saw record low share prices. In 2001 alone, more than 700 companies performed a reverse stock split.

Note that since stock splits and reverse stock splits do not change the total amount of all your investments, they should not have any taxable consequences.

STOCK TABLES

Now that we understand some of the basic elements and features of stocks, we can talk about stock tables. If you go to any exchange, you can find stock tables for specific companies. The stock table is a way of presenting pertinent information about a stock, such as bid-ask spreads, P/E ratios, dividends yields, ticker symbols, and historical share price table. Stock tables might look intimidating at first, but once you get used to them they become a nice shorthand for expressing relevant metrics.

Common metrics listed on stock tables might include:

- Stock ticker or exchange symbol
- Trading Volume - total number of share changing hands per day
- P/E ratios and earnings multiples
- Open and close bid prices for the current day
- Range - Total range of daily fluctuations in share price
- Bid-ask spread
- Dividend yield - dividend per share/share price
- 52-week highs and lows in share price

Stock tables are updated continuously with new information on daily price and volume movements. Many exchanges and broker platforms have dynamic stock tables that are constantly shifting to reflect market conditions. When you are researching potential investments, the very first thing you should look for is the stock table. That way you can get a quick overview of key pieces of information.

MARKETS AND TOOLS

Now that we have had a basic primer on the definition of stocks and important stock concepts, we can move on to the larger concepts of where to invest and how to start investing. In this chapter, we will cover the major stock exchanges and which ones are the best. We will also cover useful tools for interacting with these markets and gleaning information that is pertinent to your stock selections.

EXCHANGES

In many ways, the character of stock trading is defined by the exchange that the stocks are listed on. While it is possible to buy stock directly from a company through a direct stock purchase plan (and there are several good reasons to do so), the vast majority of stock transactions occur on the secondary markets called exchanges.

Exchanges used to be only physical places where tellers and clerks would make and fill paper orders for stock transactions. However, nowadays, exchanges can be virtual and physical. Many people still physically head to Wall St. during trading days to trade on the floor, but the vast majority of stock transactions are done through virtual networks instead of paper trails.

MAJOR STOCK EXCHANGES

The two most prominent stock exchanges in the United States are the New York Stock Exchange (NYSE) and the National Association of Securities Dealers Automated Quotations (NASDAQ or Nasdaq). Collectively, these two stock markets move hundreds of billions in capital every single day and trade billions of shares per day. These two exchanges are the largest in the world and move enormous amounts of global capital on a daily basis.

NASDAQ

The NASDAQ is the smaller of the two exchanges and is also the younger. The Nasdaq first went live in 1971 when it was founded by the entity now known as Financial Industry Regulatory Authority (FINRA). The Nasdaq was interesting because it was the world's first purely electronic stock exchange. Unlike the NYSE, the Nasdaq is purely electronic and does not have a physical location.

The Nasdaq originally was just a price quoting system and did not have a system for electronic trades until the late 70s. By the 80s, the Nasdaq had assumed the majority of over-the-counter trades (OTC), and its reputation as an OTC exchange has persisted since then. By 1981, the Nasdaq was trading approximately 37% of the US securities market for a total of 21 billion shares. It joined with the London Stock Exchange in 1992 to create the first major intercontinental linkage of trading exchanges.

For a stock to be listed on the Nasdaq, it must first be registered with the US Securities and Exchange Commission (SEC), and there need to be at least three firms that act as market makers by buying and selling the stock security at specific price quotations. Companies also have to meet specific share prices and market capitalizations. For example, shares trading under $1 are normally not listed on the Nasdaq, with a few exceptions. If a stock falls below $1, it will be delisted from the exchange if it stays under too long.

Overall, the Nasdaq has three market tiers: small-cal, mid-cap, and large-cap. Each designation refers to the total equity a company has in the exchange. Although the exact number is subject to change year to year, common parlance designates stocks with less than $2 billion as small cap, stocks with between $2 billion and $10 billion mid cap, and stocks over $10 billion large cap. Traders might refer to stocks with small market apps with other names such as micro-cap stocks, but these names are not market tiers on the Nasdaq.

New York Stock Exchange

The New York Stock Exchange is the single largest stock exchange in the world. As of 2018, the NYSE had a total market capitalization of $30 trillion, and the daily trading value exceeded $250 billion. The NYSE is a physical stock exchange and is located on 11 Wall Street and 18 Broad Street; the building itself is considered a historic landmark.

The NYSE can trace its origins back to colonial times with what was known as the Buttonwood Agreement, the earliest recorded securities trading in the colonies. Most of the early securities sold on the market were war bonds from the Revolutionary War. After some time spent changing its structure and reformations, the stock exchange moved to its current location in 1865, right near the close of the Civil War.

The invention of the telegraph is what made the NYSE a major center of commerce. The telegraph allowed essentially all of New York's exchanges to consolidate into a single center which opened up the markets to even larger flows of capital. By the late 1800s, membership had to be curtailed due to increased speculative trading.

High amounts of speculation and uncertainty plagued stock markets nearing the 20th century and the NYSE was the focal point of the infamous Black Tuesday, the day on which the stock market crashed. After the crash, the Securities Exchange Commission was formed to prevent such a crash from ever happening again and trading regulations were tightened.

Through the 21st century, the NYSE continued to grow to become the single largest stock exchange in the world. Trading is active on the floor of the exchange M-F from 9:30 am - 4:00 pm ET, except on national holidays. Traders on the floor can continuously auction for investors and take place in automated investing with wireless terminals.

The NYSE put its entire exchange online in 2007 but still allows trading in person on the floor. The exchange has become so important that it sets the routine and pace for trading around the globe. At 9:30 am, the bell rings, signaling the beginning of the trading day, and at 4:00 pm, the bell rings, signaling the close of the trading day.

NASDAQ VS. NYSE: WHICH ONE TO CHOOSE?

The main difference between the Nasdaq and the NYSE is the kind of market they are. The Nasdaq is known as a "dealers market," meaning that everyone who trades on it is trading through a dealer. In contrast, the NYSE is an auction market, which allows individuals to trade with one another. This is the most basic and obvious difference between the two, but there are others.

Auction Market vs. Dealer's Market

In an auction market, buyers and sellers submit bids to one another at competitive prices. According to the bid-ask spreads that we covered in the previous chapters, stocks trade at whatever the highest prices buyers are willing to buy. In some sense, this is the most "pure" form of stock trading because it is relatively unfettered trading between individuals (within legal regulation, of course). Auction markets may have multiple buyers and sellers simultaneously.

Contrast an auction market with a dealer's market. With a dealer's market, dealers post prices to one another to buy and sell securities. These "market makers" essentially shore up the liquidity of stocks by ensuring other dealers have a way to buy and sell shares. This method of setting market prices also allows transparency as everyone can see exactly how much a firm is willing to offer for a specific security. The structure of a dealer's market is what allows the sale of over-the-counter (OTC) shares—shares that are not listed on an official exchange. Instead, OTC shares are traded through a network of brokers and dealers rather than a centralized exchange.

One of the major results of the different structures of the NYSE and Nasdaq is how investors perceive the two. Nasdaq has a very tech-center reputation as it is the "home of the Internet" and many other hubs of innovation and technology. Tech giants such as Apple, Microsoft, Facebook, and Google all trade on the Nasdaq. As such, Nasdaq stocks are often pegged as more growth-oriented and are therefore treated as more volatile. Of course, this volatility means that you can make a fortune on the Nasdaq if you play your cards right.

Alternatively, the NYSE has been around for so long that it has become the home of some of the largest and most well-known companies in the world. For example, many large financial institutions and holding companies like JP Morgan Chase, Visa, and the famous Berkshire Hathaway of Warren Buffett trade on the NYSE. The longevity and stable reputation of the NYSE have made it home to some of the most well-known blue-chip stocks and are a home for value investors.

Nasdaq also tends to be friendly to smaller companies due to low fees for trading on the exchange. The minimum fee for listing on the Nasdaq is $55,000, and there is an annual fee of at least $43,000. As such, if you are primarily interested in small companies and micro to small-cap stocks, then the Nasdaq might be a better choice. The NYSE charges a minimum $150,000 fee for listing and an extra fee of $0.04 per share up to $295,000.

S&P 500

You may have heard the term "S&P 500" before but not known what it meant. Essentially, the S&P 500 is a particular measure of the performance of the top 500 companies on stock exchanges in the US. In other words, the S&P 500, which stands for Standards and Poor's 500, is an indicator of how the top 500 companies on any stock exchange are doing. In order to be listed on the S&P 500, companies must have a market cap of over $11.3 billion and a monthly trading volume of over 250,000 shares. The stocks must also be listed on either Nasdaq or the NYSE.

The S&P 500 contains some of the largest companies in existence, including Apple, Amazon, Microsoft, Facebook, Alphabet, Johnson & Johnson, and Berkshire Hathaway. Of the 500 companies, the top 10 make up approximately ⅓ of the total market capitalization. The S&P is known as an index that indicates the state of the top 500 companies at any given time.

The S&P 500 has been around since 1957, but its genesis goes further back than that to the 1800s. In the 1800s, Henry Poor published Poor's Publishing, an investor's guide to the railroad industry. Then in 1923, Standard Statistics introduced their mortgage ratings. Eventually, the two merged to form the Standard & Poor's 500 index.

The interesting thing about the S&P 500 is that there is a fund that is designed to track the performance of the S&P 500. It is called the SPDR S&P 500 ETF (SPY), and it allows people to buy into stock portfolios that are designed to match the performance of the S&P 500. So in other words, one of the easiest and most surefire ways to invest and take advantage of these large companies is to buy shares in the SPDR S&P 500 fund. Just like shares, units of these funds can be bought and sold on the market. We will cover mutual funds, index funds, ETFs, and more in-depth in a later chapter and discuss why they are such an excellent investment, so stay tuned.

According to expert analysts, over the past 100 years, the average annual return of the S&P 500 through its various incarnations and changing rosters is approximately 10%-11%. That means that if you had invested money over 100 years ago, it would have grown about an average of 11% per year. That is by far the best kind of investment for your money and completely blows any savings account, money market accounts, or bonds out of the water. Of course, these extraordinarily high gains have been accompanied by some big losses too. For example, the S&P 500 dropped nearly 30% over 2008 after the onset of the Great Recession.

USEFUL TOOLS FOR THE NASDAQ AND NYSE

Since the Nasdaq and NYSE are the largest exchanges in the world, you will probably spend an appreciable amount of time trading on them. So here are some of the more valuable tools for making picking investments on these exchanges easier. These are some of my favorite tools to use to vet investments and have helped me pick several winners throughout my investment career.

Finviz

Finviz is probably the single most useful free stock screener out there and has an incredible amount of free tools along with paid premium versions with advanced tools. The advanced tools are pretty neat, but you can also get a lot of fast, useful information with the free tools. Most beginners will find everything they need to screen stocks, including charts, tables, and real-time updates on price movements. The term "Finviz" is a portmanteau of "financial" and "visual" and refers to the screener's sleek, visually focused layout.

Finviz lets you search companies by ticker symbols to get a full report on current and recent past performance. When you search for a stock, it takes you to a chart that shows the 12-month performance. The basic layout that the chart uses is called a "candlestick" chart. The size of the rectangles represents the range of share price during the day, and the color red and green tell you if the stock decreased in price or increased in price for the day. Below the chart is a large table with pertinent stock info like P/E ratios, earnings, dividend yields, and other relevant performance figures.

With the free version, you can look at line charts or candlestick charts, and change time frames between daily, weekly, monthly, and intraday trades. But, if you want to do some more advanced features, then you will need to buy the subscription versions. The Elite version costs $39.50 per month or $299 per year if you opt for annual billing. You can also get your money back within 30-days so it's almost like a free 30-day trial.

Nasdaq IPO Calendar

If you are interested in investing in new companies that are just going public, then this tool will help a ton. The Nasdaq IPO calendar gives a full list of all scheduled and upcoming initial public offerings for companies on the Nasdaq, including the date, total number of shares, and expected total offer amount. For example, as of the time of writing this book, Ziprecruiter Inc and Squarespace Inc are offering IPOs on the NYSE and Nasdaq capital for 86,598,896 and 40,401,820 shares, respectively.

The Nasdaq IPO calendar also has a full list of recently completed IPOs, their total number of shares, and total offer amount. You can also find other relevant calendars from the IPO calendar, including ones for dividends, earnings, stocks splits/reverse splits, and more. This calendar is run by the Nasdaq itself, so you can be sure that all information is recent and accurate.

Trading View

TradingView is a platform if you want to look at more stock charts than you can stand. TradingView is a great resource whether you are just interested in stock or whether you are an experienced trader looking for new sources of information. TradingView has a ton of free tools on the basic account and also has paid versions for advanced analytics.

Here are just a couple of the features that TradingView offers:

- HTML5 Charts
- Server-Side Alerts
- Stock Screener
- Trading
- Analysis and Custom Tools
- Social Community of Traders
- Large Database of Articles and Educational Materials

TradingView originally started as a social platform for investors with a unique script language that allowed for charting and setting indicators. TradingView has information on the largest exchanges and foreign currency information if you want to try your hand at forex markets. The main downside of TradingView is that it doesn't integrate into most online brokerages, so you have to make trades separately.

TradingView has a free plan and three paid options:

- Pro - $14.95/month ($9.95/month annual billing)
- Pro + - $29.95/month ($19.95/month annual billing)
- Premium - $59.95/month ($39.95/month annual billing)

The free plan only gives you one chart per stock layout and only three indicators to use on that chart. You can still join the social community and look at all the research but won't get any customer support. The Pro account views up to 5 indicators per chart and no ads. However, you still only get one chart per layout.

The Pro+ plan comes with 10 chart layouts and service on up to two devices. You also get access to more advanced tracking tools. Lastly, with the Premium plan, you get the full suite of TradingView tools, up to 5 devices at once, and up to 25 indicators and 200 alerts per chart. You can also make custom indicators and superimpose them on your chart layouts.

FINAL WORDS ON STOCK EXCHANGES

Ultimately, your choice of stock exchange will probably not have an incredible amount of impact on your investing experience. However, each of the two major exchanges has some differences that make them worth checking out separately. To summarize, the Nasdaq focuses on newer, smaller stocks and tends to favor high-growth stocks in industries like tech and pharmaceutical research.

Alternatively, the NYSE is the home of the most reliable industry titans and produces value stocks from finance, utilities, and retail services. Collectively, the S&P 500 encompasses both exchanges and is an indicator of the performance of the top 500 companies at any given time.

The two exchanges also differ based on the kind of market they are in. The NYSE is an auction market, so shareholders can trade directly with one another. On the other hand, the Nasdaq is a dealer's market, meaning that large firms establish liquidity by offering to buy and sell shares from a particular company.

These key facts are the most important things that you need to know about the major exchanges. In the next chapter, we will give a more thorough view of stock exchange, and cover sectors, indices, index funds/ETFs, and the concept of income stocks, and why they are an amazing choice for your retirement portfolio.

OTHER TYPES OF INVESTMENT VEHICLES

So far, we have covered the major points of stocks, stock markets, and the different types of exchanges. In this chapter, we will go more in-depth on the different ins and outs of the stock market, including sectors, indices, and other types of investments aside from just stocks and shares. We will finish the chapter by introducing the concept of income stocks and how to properly choose income stocks for your portfolio.

SECTORS, INDUSTRIES, AND INDICES

If you frequent stock and trading message boards, you might hear people talking about certain "sectors" doing well or performing poorly. What is a sector in the stock market, and why are they important?

In short terms, a sector is just a specific part of the stock market and the companies wherein. Usually, sectors are divided based on the kinds of companies that make them up. The reason why sectors are important is because companies in the same sectors are subject to the same pressures and competition, and specific occurrences can drastically affect the state of an entire sector. Moreover, you can look at sectors to get an accurate view of the current state of an industry.

In the US stock markets, there are 11 commonly used sectors that can be defined by the kinds of products and services that the companies provide. They are:

1. **Information Technologies.** The IT sector includes companies that disseminate tech services and computer-related tech such as computers, OSs, processors, microchips, etc. Companies in the IT sectors include tech giants like Microsoft and Apple.
2. **Health Care.** The healthcare industry encompasses a wide range of products and services ranging from health care providers, health insurance companies, medical tech developers, pharmaceuticals and drug research, and biotech companies. Cannabis companies are a popular up-and-comer in the health care sector.
3. **Financials.** Financials include big banks and lending institutions such as JP Morgan Chase, Visa, Wells Fargo, Bank of America, Goldman Sachs, etc. These companies are involved in financial services and products like credit cards, bank accounts, mortgages, and holding companies. The Financials sector has some of the most well-established and oldest companies in the country.
4. **Consumer Discretionary.** Consumer discretionary sector covers products and luxury items that are inessential. Things like jewelry, cars, clothing, consumer electronic devices, and other luxury

expenses like hospitality and restaurants. The consumer sector is probably one of the more broadly defined sectors in the market.

5. **Communications.** Communication includes companies that offer phone and internet services, as well as major telecommunications and media companies. Netflix and Walt Disney Co. are some of the largest companies that are in this sector, as well as large-cap mainstays like AT&T, Comcast, Verizon, and more.

6. **Industrial.** The industrial sector includes a large range of companies that deal with heavy materials and the transportation of those materials. Things like airlines, railways, weapons manufacturers, and shipping companies. Some of the larger companies included in this sector include Delta, Boeing, FedEx, and Southwest Airlines.

7. **Consumer Staples.** Consumer staples include companies that provide necessities and other basic amenities for living. Grocery stores, large retail chains, household products, and personal health and wellness products are included in this sector. Some of the larger companies include Johnson & Johnson, Kroger, Procter & Gamble, as well as Dawn.

8. **Energy.** Energy stocks are self-explanatory and include those companies that play a role in the energy infrastructure. Oil, coal, natural gas, and consumable extractor companies, as well as companies that refine these kinds of materials, are considered energy. The energy sector holds some of the largest companies in the entire world by earnings, including oil and energy magnates Exxon Mobil and Chevron.

9. **Utilities.** The Utility sector includes all companies that provide things like power, sewage, and water to residents and businesses. Utility companies tend to be very stable and provide excellent dividends as they have a constant source of cash flow from customer subscriptions and monthly statements. Big utility companies to check out include Duke, AEP, Pacific Gas & Electric, and Consolidated Edison.

10. **Real Estate.** Real estate includes everything related to land and housing development, inducing construction, real estate investment trusts (REITs), realtor services, and more. The real estate sector is very large and makes up almost 3% of the S&P 500 on its own. Some of the larger companies in real estate include American Tower

Corp, Equinix, American Realty Investors, and Simon Property Group.

11. **Raw Materials.** Lastly, the raw materials sector includes all companies that extract raw materials that need to be processed for other sectors to use. Companies that handle things like mining gold, iron, copper, and zinc, as well as forestry companies, are large contenders in this sector. Container and packaging companies are often included in the raw materials sector as well. Big names in the raw materials sector include metal-mining company Rio Tinto and plastic manufacturer Lyondellbasell.

These 11 sectors are the most common division, but you can dice sectors up as fine-grained as you want, depending on your needs. For example, you could narrow your analysis to specifically the plastics industry or the computer processors sector. Whether you take a coarse-grained approach to define sectors or a more fine-grained approach depends on your investment goals.

Under the division of sector is "industry." These two terms are often used interchangeably, but they have different meanings. A sector is a loose grouping of major businesses. At the same time, industries are more narrow and defined by the primary line of business. Industries can get more and more fine-grained, depending on your level of analysis.

Both sectors can have indices, which we explained in an earlier chapter, and are measures of a particular performance of a portion of the stock exchange. Various sector indices include the Dow Jones Industrial Average, Capitalization weighted index, and the Russell 200, which is composed entirely of the highest trading small-cap businesses.

WHY ARE SECTORS AND INDUSTRIES IMPORTANT?

Sectors are important for three major reasons.

First, looking at a sector can give you a good bird's eye view of how that sector, in general, is doing. For example, say you wanted to know whether investing in oil and natural gas would be a good idea for your portfolio. If the oil and gas sector is doing well as a whole, then that is a positive first sign that investing in oil and gas could do well for you.

At the same time, when sectors are doing poorly, that gives you a quick list of companies that it may be best to hold off investing in for now. Of course, these are just general rules of thumb. A sector may be doing poorly as a whole, but investing in a company in that sector might still be a good idea.

Another reason why sectors are important is because they form useful explanatory units to explain market movements. For example, legislation surrounding carbon emissions would presumably affect the entire oil and gas industry. Similarly, legislation affecting banking regulations would also have a predictable effect on the financial sector and investment and retail banking sectors.

MUTUAL FUNDS AND INDEX FUNDS

Lastly, sectors, industries, and indices are very important because they give funds specific targets to match their performance too. We mentioned the famous SPDR S&P 500 fund in the last chapter and how it matches its performance to the S&P 500 index. There are various funds that are indexed to sector indices to match their overall rate of return.

In the investment world, a **mutual fund** is a type of investment vehicle in which multiple investors will pool their money to buy several investments. Investors into the fund receive a portion of returns proportional to their initial investment. Mutual funds are a way for you to invest in multiple companies all at once without buying individual shares in those companies.

When you invest in a mutual fund, a *fund manager* handles the minutiae of the investments and takes a small % fee as compensation. This fee is calculated based on what is known as the **expense ratio** of the fund. The expense ratio of a fund is simply the ratio of operating costs relative to the total assets of the fund.

A fund with an expense ratio of 0.5%, for example, would take 0.5% of the earnings of any investment as a fee for management. So, for example, if a fund earned $3000 in a year with a 0.5% expense ratio, you would pay $15 in annual fees.

Sectors indices and mutual funds go hand in hand because sectors give funds a target to match their performance too. For example, the SPDR S&P 500 mutual fund is composed of shares of the companies on the S&P 500 index and is arranged to match its annual return with that of the index. This method of tracking indices is what gives funds their investment power and why they historically can generate such high returns. Mutual funds that are meant to track specific indices are called **index funds**.

Index funds are an excellent way to diversify your investments. Index funds run best when they are composed of a diverse range of companies and investments. Any lag or subpar performance in one area will be compensated for by the performance in another area.

Index funds are also **passively managed,** meaning that they are automatically set to follow an index and are not actively managed by an investor. The passive nature of index tracker funds means that they have low costs, and you do not have to micromanage them yourself. The average expense ratio of passively managed index funds is around 0.02%, which is equivalent to $2 per every $1,000 of earnings.

There are other kinds of mutual funds that may or may not be passively managed. **Actively managed** funds are ones that are continuously monitored by a group of investment experts to meet certain target metrics. Actively managed funds are constantly being updated or modified depending on the state of the underlying investments. As such, actively managed funds tend to have higher expense ratios in the 0.5%-1.0% range.

ETFs

Exchange-traded funds (ETFs) are a special kind of mutual fund that gets a lot of attention and for a good reason. ETFs are the same as most mutual funds in that they are made out of pools of investments and represent several companies or sectors. Like mutual funds, ETFs can passively track an index, or they can be actively managed. You can think of them as little "baskets" of investments.

The special feature of ETFs is that you can buy and sell ETFs on the stock market just like individual shares. You cannot do this with mutual funds. ETFs are funds that behave like shares and are associated with the volatility and liquidity of individual shares with the diversification and stability of a mutual fund.

ETFs are often considered a safe bet for new investors because they combine the features of both stocks and funds. You can trade individual units of ETFs like stock, but each unit is composed of a range of diversified assets, including stocks, bonds, commodities, cash products, and more. The famous S&P 500 fund that we keep mentioning is an indexed ETF that can be bought and sold on the market just like shares.

Also, unlike mutual funds who only change value at the close of a trading day, ETFs constantly fluctuate in value over the day. They are often a better choice for beginner investors than other kinds of mutual funds because they have relatively low expense ratios, low investment thresholds, and are highly liquid on the market.

Within ETFs, there are several distinct subtypes, mostly differentiated by the underlying asset classes the fund focuses on. For example:

- Bond ETFs typically feature bonds and other low-risk, fixed-income securities like treasury bonds and corporate bonds.
- Industry ETFs feature a portion of specific industries, like tech, oil, pharmaceuticals, gas, or internet providers.
- Commodities ETFs focus on investing in things like gold, crude oil, agricultural products, and other physical goods with use-value.
- Currency ETFs are composed of various foreign currencies, including GBP, EUR, CAD, JPY, CHF (Swiss Franc), and AUD.

You can buy ETFs just like you would any other kind of share. You search for them on the market, and then you can select how many units you want to buy.

Here is a list of some of the top ETFs in the stock market and their focus.

- Ethereum Cryptocurrencies
- S&P 500 Energy Sector
- Morningstar MLP Composite
- MSCI World Financials
- Palladium
- Vanguard Mid-Cap ETF
- S&P Commodity Producers Agribusiness

PROS AND CONS OF ETFS

ETFs are often touted as a good investment for first-time stock traders. But, like any investment, they have their pros and cons.

Pros

- **Diversification.** One of the best reasons to invest in ETFs is that they are highly diversified by nature and give you good market coverage.
- **Liquid.** For the most part, ETFs trade just like shares, and they tend to be highly liquid. Their prices update throughout the day too.
- **Low expense ratios.** Most ETFs are passively managed, so they are a relatively cheap option for a fund.
- **More tax-efficient.** ETFs might be more tax-efficient than other mutual funds in many cases because they do not require capital gains to be immediately distributed to holders.

Cons

- **More volatile.** Because they trade like stocks and are highly liquid, ETFs can be more volatile than other kinds of mutual and indexed funds.
- **More expensive than shares.** ETFs are reasonably cheap, but they are still more costly than individual shares that do not have any expense ratios.
- **Lower dividend yields.** If you are a dividend investor, then ETFs might not be the ideal choice because they generate relatively fewer dividends than other kinds of investments.

INCOME STOCKS

For many investors, the goal of investing is to find shares that you can buy, and then they will increase in value. Most people think of the capital appreciation angle to investing when they think of making a lot of money in the stock market.

However, stocks can pay in other ways besides capital gains. **Income stocks** are stocks and securities that generate a steady stream of income in addition to appreciating in value. Income stocks pay dividends to investors, so they get a steady stream of income.

We have mentioned dividends elsewhere, but **dividends** are basically a portion of the company's earnings that gets paid directly to investors. Unlike capital gains, dividends do not need to be realized by a sale and are automatically distributed to shareholders every financial quarter. You can think of dividends as a bit like interest in that you generate small periodic fixed cash payments from your investments.

Stocks that produce a lot of dividends are known as income stocks. There is no official cutoff, but income stocks are stocks that have a higher than average *dividend yield*. Dividend yield can be calculated as the total amount of dividends produced per share by the price per share. For example, if some stock pays out $4 in dividends per share and the current share price is $120, then those shares have a ($4/$120) x 100 = 3% dividend yield.

Features of Income Stocks

Many investors planning for retirement favor income stocks because they can provide a solid stream of liquid cash to live on during retirement. Income stocks tend to be in those industries that produce steady returns and that do not fluctuate much over the year.

What is and isn't a "good" income stock depends on the needs of the specific investors. But generally, experts say that a dividend yield of 4% is considered good. It is also a good sign if companies have managed to increase dividend distributions year after year. For example, Coca-Cola has managed to increase dividend distributions for investors every year for 60 years straight.

Wal-Mart is another dividend giant and has increased dividend yields for the past 30 years.

What Sectors Have Good Income Stocks?

As a general rule of thumb, the best companies for income and dividend stocks are the ones that have a high cash flow. When companies operate in the positive for cash, that means they have more money to dole out as dividend distributions. The companies that have the highest cash flows are the ones that offer some kind of staple product or service that everyone needs and that generates a lot of money shifting hands.

Many companies in the utility sector are known for paying high dividends. This is because utilities by their nature are resilient and somewhat recession-proof. Even when the general economy is bad, no one is going to stop paying for gas or electricity, so they manage constant stable performance and are highly resilient to a general economic downturn. Utility companies also generate a ton of cash in service payments from customers so they can pass on a good chunk of that change to investors before putting profits back into operations.

Telecommunications companies like At&T and Comcast are also good candidates for income stocks for the same reason. They have massive stores of cash and a nearly ubiquitous presence in modern life. And last, consumer staple stores like Kroger, Walgreens, and CVS are frequently ranked among the best and most stable dividend stocks, with dividend yield routinely reaching as high as 6%-7%.

Income stocks can be matched with growth and value stocks as another major kind of stock to keep on your radar. Out of the three, income stocks tend to be the least volatile and the most reliable; they also tend to generate the least in non-dividend returns, though this is not necessarily always true. Some income stocks manage to pay a great dividend and have excellent growth and value.

At this point, you should have a thorough grasp of the different kinds of investments and how they work. In the next chapter, we will dig deeper into the question of how, precisely, to analyze stocks and what methods you can use to pick winning investments.

FUNDAMENTAL AND TECHNICAL ANALYSIS

So now that you understand the major kinds of investment vehicles, as well as the more detailed features of stocks and shares, we can talk about how to go about picking stocks for your portfolio.

Traditionally, most investors use one of two major kinds of analysis to evaluate stocks and determine if they are a good choice to buy or sell. The two kinds of analysis are called **fundamental** and **technical analysis.**

FUNDAMENTAL ANALYSIS

Of the two major methods of market analysis, fundamental analysis is probably the more widespread and easier to learn about. Fundamental analysis is all about gauging the **intrinsic value** of stocks. We have mentioned intrinsic value beforehand, but now we can go more in-depth. The intrinsic value of a stock is the objective value of a particular security conceptually distinct from the current trading value of the security.

According to this idea of intrinsic value, it is possible for there to be a mismatch between the intrinsic value of a stock and the current trading price of that stock. As such, stocks trading under their intrinsic value would be considered undervalued, and stocks trading over their intrinsic value would be overvalued.

Remember, a key part of value investing and finding value stocks is finding stocks that are trading at a share price below what their intrinsic value would suggest. Suppose a company is trading below what its intrinsic value would suggest. In that case, the company might be due for growth when the price corrects. If the share price is higher than what intrinsic value would suggest, it could signify that the shares will soon face a contraction when the trading price corrects and contracts.

Intrinsic value can be calculated in several ways, and every analyst will bring a unique lens to the table when calculating intrinsic value. As such, gauging intrinsic value is a partially subjective process, and there is no one "right" way to do it, per se. Analysts will include various things that could affect intrinsic value into their models, including qualitative, quantitative, and other factors.

Since there is no one way to do fundamental analysis, there is no simple equation you can plug things into to figure out the intrinsic value. However, there are several key features, tools, and metrics of stocks that inform analysts' fundamental analyses.

Net Profit

In normal parlance, the profit of a company is what is leftover from gross revenue once all debts have been paid. It's the "extra" bit left over after the business accounts for all of its liabilities and the entire point of business in the first place. Net profit after taxes gives you a good indication of how the company's handling their overheads and what kinds of advantages they have over other companies.

Profit Margins

However, net profits might not tell the whole story. High earnings are good, but they might be offset by the high costs for generating those earnings. Hence, profit margins refer to the ratio of the total profit that a business squeezes out of every dollar they spend. You can calculate profit margins with a simple equation by dividing net income by revenue.

Profit margin = (Net profit/Revenue) x 100

If a company has higher profit margins, then that means they have a better handle and control over their costs and can squeeze more value out of every dollar they spend. A company might make a ton of profit in an absolute sense but still have relatively thin profit margins. For example, say a company makes a net profit of $2.82 billion of a total revenue spread of $21 billion. The profit margin would be ($2.82 billion/21 billion) x 100 = **13.4%**

Price to Earnings Ratio

We have already talked about price-to-earnings ratios before, and they are a key item in fundamental analysis. To recap, the price-to-earnings ratio of some shares is equal to the total price per share divided by the total earnings per share. P/E ratios can tell you whether a company is cheap or expensive relative to the earnings it produces. P/E ratios can be compared with historical P/E data or be calculated on projected future earnings estimates.

Price to Book Value

Book value is an extremely important concept in fundamental analysis and refers to the total cost of carrying an asset. In other words, book values are basically a measure of the net asset value of a company and can be calculated by subtracting the total liabilities of a company from its total assets.

Liabilities include anything the company might owe, such as wages, interest, salaries, bond payments, or fixed and variable expenses. This remaining number is then divided by the total number of common shares to get the book value per share of a company.

So, for example, say you look at the stock table for a company and calculate that their total assets are $20 billion and total liabilities equal $7 billion. The book value of the company is a simple calculation: $20 billion - $7 billion = $13 billion. If the company currently has 300 million outstanding shares, then the book value per share of the company would be ($13 billion/ 300 million shares) = $43.33 per share.

Then, you can take that book value and compare it to the actual trading price of the security by calculating the Price to Book ratio (P/B ratio). Divide the current market price per share by the book value per share. A low P/B ratio indicates that a share is selling at below the book value and potentially is undervalued. A high P/B ratio suggests that shares are trading at a higher amount than the net asset value per share, and might be overvalued and facing a pending price contraction and correction.

Return on Equity

Another popular metric for measuring intrinsic value is the return on equity value. Return on equity value refers to the ratio of profit to shareholder equity and can be calculated by dividing the net profit of a company by the total shareholder equity. Shareholder equity is equal to the total assets minus liabilities. For example, if a company recorded a net profit of $2 billion and had total shareholder equity of $20 billion, then the return on equity for those shares would be 10%.

Return on equity tells you how efficient the company is at generating profits and paying its debtors. It can tell you whether a company owes a lot of money to some party, and it can tell you the expected return you would see if you invested in those shares. In general, you want to look at companies that outperform their peers in their sector.

HOW TO DO FUNDAMENTAL ANALYSIS

Fundamental analysis is not an exact science, and there is no one way to do it. Whether an investment is a good call or not depends on your specific investment goals, preferences, and risk tolerance. What this means is that no single tool or method used in fundamental analysis will give you a complete answer on whether you should buy or sell some stock. Any fundamental metric needs to be contextualized on other numbers and data.

Analysts might also include other more qualitative features when calculating intrinsic value. Other aspects that might be factored into a fundamental analysis include things like:

- Management experience
- Employee education and experience
- Reputation and public goodwill
- Company enthusiasm
- Company history and current events
- Shareholder confidence

The trick is that many things that cannot be readily quantified will have an effect on the company's intrinsic value. For example, the CEO of a company involved in a major scandal could affect the company's intrinsic value and might be factored into a fundamental analysis.

So, when it comes to making your own fundamental analysis, you can add in features that seem more subjective. Ultimately, the intrinsic value depends on the inventor that is making the assessment.

TECHNICAL ANALYSIS

In contrast to fundamental analysis, which is based around looking at fundamental pricing features of stocks, technical analysis is about using mathematical methods and historical data to predict future price movements. Whereas fundamental analysis is the "classic" golden form of investing, technical analysis is its sleeker, novel, silver cousin.

Technical analysis is distinguished from other forms of analysis due to its heavy reliance on statistics and relative downplaying of the intrinsic character of specific investments. In that sense, technical analysis focuses most on purely quantitative features of investments, such as price movement and trading volumes. If you are more mathematically inclined and enjoy looking at stock charts and graphs all day, then technical analysis might be a good evaluation methodology for you to try.

Technical analysis is about using math to determine how supply and effect will affect changes in price, volume, and volatility. It is based on a key principle that past price and volume movements can give reliable indicators about future price movements and volumes. There are literally thousands of technical indicators you can calculate, but virtually all of them can be divided into about 5 major categories.

- **Trends.** Whether a stock is moving up or down
- **Mean reversion.** How far prices will swing before being corrected
- **Relative strength indexes.** Oscillations in pressures to buy and sell
- **Momentum.** Speed and amount of change over time
- **Volume.** Quantity of trades

Additionally, most types of indicators can be considered either lagging or leading. Lagging indicators use past information to determine why the share price is currently, while leading indicators attempt to project future price movements.

Moving Averages

A moving average is a very simple trend indicator that tells you the average price of a security over a given time span. If you look at any price chart, you will see that it is very spiky and goes up and down jaggedly. Calculating the moving average is a mathematical technique that smooths out that pricing data into a line to see how the average price of a security is moving over time and whether it is trending positive or negative.

Averages are taken over specific units of time, whether it's a few days, weeks, months, or years. Simply add the average stock price of a security over some period of time, and then divide that amount by the total number of units of time. A simple moving average is calculated by taking flat pricing data and doing simple division.

Moving averages can be calculated over any time frame, but the most common ranges are 50, 100, and 200 days. These measures are very easy to calculate and give you a decent impression of price movements over the past few weeks to months. You can even compare moving averages to see how they crossover one another. A common strategy is to plot a 50-day moving average against a 200-day average and look for where the 50-day line crosses over the 200-day line as a buy signal.

Keep in mind that moving averages on their own cannot necessarily predict the future movement of prices but only tells you what the average price is doing over some period of time.

In addition to simple moving averages, there are also *exponential moving averages* (EMAs). EMAs are calculated similarly to simple moving averages but puts more weight on more recent dates. EMAs are used because new price movement data is considered more relevant than older price movement data. Moist chatting tools have some kind of calculator for creating exponential moving averages.

Bollinger Bands

Bollinger Bands are a mean reversion indicator that is supposed to tell you how far prices oscillate from a central tendency point. Bollinger bands appear on a stock chart as two thick, bolded lines that enclose a simple moving average. Basically, the Bollinger bands tell you the average fluctuates around a central price.

Calculating Bollinger bands is a bit involved. First, you need to calculate a simple moving average, most often a 20-day moving average. Next, find the difference in price between each data point and the moving average, square the results, and add them all together. Then, divide this number by the total number of data points. Last, take the square root of the resultant number, and multiply by 2. Add that amount to the moving average line and you have the top band. Subtract that amount from the moving average and you will have the bottom band.

Bollinger Bands are very popular because they are believed to show resistance to price movements. If the bands are relatively narrow, then it means that the price was less volatile during that time and hovered closer to the average. When bands move close together, this is called the *squeeze* and is considered to be a sign of future volatility. So if you calculate Bollinger Bands and notice a squeeze is occurring, that could mean there will be a future increase in volatility.

MACD

The MACD (Moving average convergence divergence) is a momentum indicator that is used to analyze rapid changes in prices. MACD shows a relationship between two moving averages. The MACD can be calculated by subtracting the long-term exponential moving average from the short-term exponential moving average. Long-term EMAs are usually calculated over 26 periods, and short-term EMAs are calculated over 12 periods. The MACD is positive when the short-term EMA is above the long-term EMA and negative when the short-term EMA is below the long-term EMA.

The MACD is seen as measuring the tendency for the price to move in one direction, relative to a defined baseline. The baseline is up to your choice and might be based on simple moving averages of some other kind of metric. The higher the MACD line is above the baseline, the further apart the short-term and long-term EMAs are growing apart.

Relative Strength Index (RSI)

The relative strength index (RSI) is an oscillating indicator that measures buying and selling pressures for some security. It measures price changes to determine whether a security is currently being overbought or oversold.

Essentially, the RSI tells you how much of a security is being bought or sold at gains or losses. The RSI line will rise if there are more and larger positive closes and will fall the more and larger losses there are over that same period. The further an RSI line trends up, the more the security can be considered overbought. Conversely, when the RSI line is in a downtrend, then that means the security might be oversold.

RSI ratings are also used to tell whether a market is bearish or bullish. Bearish markets are signified by a fear of loss, and there is a sentiment that prices will soon fall. In contrast, a bullish market sees a lot of buying behavior, and the general sentiment is that investments will rise.

Parabolic SAR

One last important technical indicator I want to cover is the parabolic SAR. The parabolic SAR is a momentum indicator that is used to determine the direction of price movements and suitable entry and exit points. It is sometimes called the "stop and reversal system." The parabolic SAR appears as a series of dots that sit above and below the price bars. Dots on top of the price bars indicate that the price is bearish and might decrease, while dots below the bar are seen as bullish and the price might increase.

The key thing about the Parabolic SAR is that it can show the ideal entry and exit point during price reversals. As the price continues to increase, the dots go higher and get further apart. Taking advantage of these swing points can help you net profit and staunch any losses, but parabolic SARs can be misleading in a ranging market where there is not much price movement momentum. In cases where there is not much momentum, it is easy to fall to false signals of price movements.

HOW TO DO TECHNICAL ANALYSIS

Most of the time, there will be too much data available for you to calculate technical indicators by hand. That is why most stock charts and screening tools have built-in technical indicators that you can toss up and superimpose on the stock chart data. More advanced stock screening tools will give you the tools to define your own technical indicators so you can experiment.

There are two main approaches to doing technical analysis. Top-down and bottom-up. The top-down approach starts at the widest level of resolution of the economy and slowly analyzes down into specific sectors and industries. The global view that a top-down approach gives lets you indicate macroeconomic trends, which might be signs of activity in smaller markets.

Bottom-up approaches tend to start at the ground level of individual shares and investments rather than at a macroeconomic level. Bottom-up processes tend to focus on identifying entry and exit points and specific trends in data rather than global trends. Since bottom-up investors start at the individual stock level, they are more invested in finding good candidates for long-term holding.

One of the key things with technician analysis is to not put all your faith in a single indicator. Indicators only tell you a part of the picture, and no indicator by itself can accurately predict how the market will go. The key is to find a strategy that works for you, and that does not overstep any risk tolerances that you have. On the other side, you do not want to overload your chart data with a bunch of irrelevant technical indicators. Pick a handful that you get a good intuitive feel for and craft your investing strategy around those.

As is the case with fundamental analysis, there is no one "right" way to do technical analysis. You can often combine aspects of both fundamental and technical analysis to create hybrid trading strategies. In fact, the best strategies combine the time-tested methods of fundamental analysis with the mathematical elegance and sophistication of technical analysis.

TRADING STRATEGIES

So far, we have covered the basics of stocks, different types of investments, the different sectors of the market, how to analyze investments, and different concepts for analyzing price movements and financial metrics. Now it's time to get into actual trading strategies. In this chapter, we will cover various trading strategies and talk about what makes them work and how you can incorporate them into your investment plan.

We will start simple and move our way to the move complex topics and strategies.

TYPES OF TRADING STRATEGIES

There are two major types of investing strategies, and we have already talked about them a bit previously: **passive** and **active.**

Passive Investing

Passive trading or passive investing is a relatively hands-off investment strategy meant to hold on to long-term gains. The whole point of passive investing is to minimize your buying and selling behavior with a buy-and-hold mentality. Passive investing is low-cost and relatively low-effort as you don't have to spend time micromanaging your portfolios and making daily trades.

The best example of a passive approach to investing is probably an index fund like we covered in the previous chapter. Index funds are designed to match the composition of the index they are tracking. Whenever the index changes, these kinds of funds automatically change their composition to update. This rearranging is done automatically without your input. Index funds are an excellent method of passive investing as you can stick your money in a fund and leave it alone while periodically adding more.

The entire point of passive investing is to build wealth gradually over time. Passive investors should thus be oriented to long-term horizons and should not be in it to make money quickly. Since the entire point of passive investing is to keep your hands off your money as much as possible, there are relatively few explicit "strategies" for passive investing.

Roboadvisors

One of the best options for passive investors is the roboadvisor. Roboadvisors are basically investment platforms that automate some or all of your trading. The term "advisor" is a bit misleading as the robot doesn't advise anyone; it just automates the investment process. With a roboadvisor, you can define your preferred portfolio allocations and composition, and the roboadvisor algorithm will automatically buy and sell assets to maintain those allocations.

For example, say you want to keep your allocations at 40% bonds and 60% shares. If your allocations drift out of those ranges, the roboadvisor will automatically buy and sell assets to get back to that allocation.

Roboadvisors are probably the ultimate tool for passive investing as you can just stick your money in one and basically forget about it. Roboadvisors are built using sophisticated algorithms based on modern economic theory, specifically **Modern Portfolio Theory (MPT)**, as created by Nobel Laureate Harry Markowitz. MPT provides a mathematical framework that allows you to minimize the risk of assets while maximizing the returns of your portfolio for a given risk level. The basic tack of MPT is that individual investment performance is not as important as how much that individual investment affects the risk/reward ratio of your portfolio.

MPT uses some very complicated mathematical and statistical techniques. We won't get into the nitty-gritty details; however, the basic idea is that the overall expected return of the portfolio is calculated as a weighted average of the expected returns of the individual investments. The bottom line is that roboadvisors invest according to this cutting-edge economic theory so that you can feel confident in roboadvisor portfolio performance.

Dollar-Cost Averaging

Dollar-cost averaging is another popular form of passive investment. Dollar-cost averaging (DCA) involves splitting your investments up over a time frame to reduce your capital exposure to risk. Dollar-cost averaging is often touted as a good investment strategy for those who want to take the emotion out of investing, as it requires you to stick to a consistent schedule and discourages you from trying to "time" the market.

Here is a simple example of how DA works. Say you have $1,000, and you want to buy 100 shares at $10 a share. One option is to just buy all those shares at once. Dollar-cost averaging involves splitting up that investment into pieces over time. For example, say you split that purchase up into 5 equal-sized pieces, so you buy 20 shares at a time over 5 weeks.

Time Interval	Amount	Share Price	No. Purchase Shares
1 week	$200	$10	20
2 week	$200	$10	20
3 week	$200	$6	33
4 week	$200	$7	28
5 week	$200	$9	22
Final	**$1,000**	**$8.4 - avg. cost per share**	**123**

Here is what would have happened if you had bought all those shares at once:

Time Interval	Amount	Share Price	No. Purchase Shares
1 week	$1,000	$10	100
2 week	$0	$10	0
3 week	$0	$6	0
4 week	$0	$7	0
5 week	$0	$9	0
Final	**$1,000**	**$10 - avg. cost per share**	**100**

Notice that when you did DCA, you ended up with more shares and paid less on average per share. The basic idea behind DCA is that you can split up your principle into smaller chunks to take advantage of these kinds of price movements.

DCA is considered a passive form of investing as it can be done automatically and is not sensitive to market conditions. It takes the emotion out of investing, so you don't panic buy and sell if performance starts to falter.

Active Investing

In contrast to passive investing is active investing. Whereas passive investing is as hands-off as possible, active investing involves active management of your portfolio. Active investors try to time their investments and arrange their portfolios to beat the market and make higher than average returns.

There is still some debate over how effective active trading strategies are. Many argue that the stock market is inherently unpredictable, and active trading strategies fare no better than buy-and-hold strategies. Others are more optimistic and think that active trading can help you beat the market.

What is true is that there are many successful active investors who make a living day trading and micromanaging their portfolio to get as much profit as possible. There are essentially infinite active trading strategies, but we wanted to focus on 4 key strategies that most beginner inventors should understand.

Position Trading

Position trading is considered the "standard' investment approach and involves seeking out investments that will appreciate over time. Position trading is probably the least "active" of active trading strategies and shares a lot in common with forms of passive investing.

Position trading is based on the idea that, all other things being equal, trends in the market are likely to continue into the future. It is here that position traders can be distinguished from the passive investing buy-and-hold approach. Position traders are trying to identify and take advantage of trends and will wait for a peak time to sell. The position trader can hold for a long period of time, but their ultimate goal is to ride a trend out and sell at the max.

Position trading is about identifying the right entry and exit points for a particular sale. To that end, position traders use all kinds of techniques, including fundamental analysis and technical analysis. Position traders might use fundamental analysis to identify highly undervalued companies that they expect to rise in value.

For example, a common position trading strategy is using support and resistance to time entry and exits. A support level refers to the price that an asset will not fall below, while the resistance is the point after which the price will not rise. Support and resistance levels can be gauged by the historical price of the stock or at previous support levels. Position traders can use a method called "Fibonacci retracement" to find support and resistance points.

To do Fibonacci retracement, take the segment of the stock chart you want to analyze and draw a horizontal line labeled 100% at the highest price point and another horizontal line labeled 0% at the lowest price point. Next, draw in 4 more lines at 61.8%, 50%, 38.2%, and 23.6%. These lines might look random, but they are based on the golden ratio, which is intimately related to natural growth processes. These lines can be used as a rough guide for support and resistance levels to time entry and exit points in the market. (Most trading platforms do this for you.)

One of the major weaknesses of position trading is that, very often, trends in the market do not hold. An unexpected trend reversal might upset position trading plans and incur a loss. Since position traders buy for trends, their capital might be locked up for longer periods of time.

Day Trading

In contrast to position trading, day trading focuses on short-term gains and seeks to close out a position at the end of every trading day. Day traders typically only hold onto assets for a few hours and try to take advantage of short-term fluctuations in price to make a profit. Day trading is very risky as price points can be highly volatile during the day.

Most day traders rely on technical analysis to simplify the massive amounts of stock data that comes in every day. Day traders are concerned mostly with price movements rather than business fundamentals, so technical analysis is a natural fit for the trading style. Simplifying decisions to price movement concerns lets you trade more efficiently.

One of the most important technical indicators that day traders can use is volume indicators. Rember, volume is the total number of shares changing hands on the market. A very high trading volume indicates high liquidity, which is often accompanied by price movements. For example, if a day trader suddenly notices a high volume of buys, that could be an indicator that the price is going to rise.

Day traders can also identify trend lines by connecting the highs and lows of stocks with diagonal lines. Day traders also make use of support and resistance lines. For example, it is common for day traders to use a 200-day simple moving average as a baseline support. Keep in mind that day traders can support technical analysis with fundamentals. For example, if there is a breakout for a stock, but the company's earnings statement has fallen from the last quarter, that could be a signal to take a short position.

One major drawback of day trading is just how risky it is. On smaller and smaller time frames, stock movements become basically random, so it can be very hard to separate genuine trend signals from false signals and noise. This is one major reason why many long-term investors think day trading is ultimately a losing battle and is as effective as guessing.

Swing Trading

Swing trading occupies a nice middle ground between position trading and long trading and tries to capitalize on medium-term gains in the market. Swing traders might hold a position for a few days or weeks rather than just a day or months. Given that they are focused on smaller time frames, swing traders often use technical analysis to time entry and exit points. In many ways, day trading and swing trading are the same; the main difference is the time frame of holdings.

However, one very important difference between the two is that the swing traders will hold assets overnight. This opens up the swing trader to overnight risk and gaps up and down in their position.

One of the more useful tools for a swing trader is candlestick charts. These charts show the volume and direction of price movements throughout a day. Candlesticks can be used to identify support and resistance bars. In general, the best types of stocks for swing trading tend to be large-cap stocks that have high liquidity and trading volumes.

Scalping

Scalping is a particular method of day trading that seeks to profit off small changes in pricing. Scalping is a lot like day trading but even more so. Scalpers are trying to profit off tiny changes in prices. This means that they often take out large numbers of positions with the idea that they can make a lot from a bunch of tiny wins. For example, imagine that the share price only rises by $0.03. If you have 100,000 shares, then that would be again of nearly $3,000 in a single day.

Scalping also involves having a solid exit strategy. One bad loss could potentially wipe out all the small gains you made through the day. That is why scalpers trade in the shortest time frames possible. Some scalpers open a position for literally minutes or seconds before closing out.

USING A SCREENER TOOL FOR TRADING STRATEGIES

An invaluable tool for devising trading strategies is a stock screener. Stock screeners allow you to sift through the massive amounts of stock data so you can find selections that fit your investment preferences. I personally like www.finviz.com, but you can use any of them. Here are some good parameters to pin in the stock screener that will be useful for finding good selections.

- Change the market cap to over $2 billion. This will cut out all micro-cap companies and leave you with strong companies with staying power and presence.
- Change average share volume to 500,000. You want to be looking for stocks that have high liquidity and potential for price changes.
- Try looking for individual shares and ETFs mostly. These are highly liquid and can be traded throughout the day.
- Change the share price to at least $10. Penny stocks can be a way to make money, but they are highly risky and usually not worth the investment.
- Set the IPO date to at least 3 years ago. Typically most companies make their biggest moves in the first 3 years after they go public.
- Expected earnings per share growth over the next year should be at least 20%
- . We want to find companies that are actually growing year after year.
- Sales growth quarter over quarter should be over 20%. We want companies that have a steady growth in their revenues.
- Lastly, set a technical indicator for a 20, 50, and 200-day moving average to identify stocks that are in a genuine uptrend.

Once you have some good parameters set for your screener, sort everything by volume and look at these stocks for potential breakouts. The list will show you extreme high momentum stocks that are making high growth and have a good future ahead of them.

5 ECONOMIC FORCES THAT AFFECT THE STOCK MARKET

P eople often talk about the stock market and economy as if they are, in fact, one and the same. This is not true. The stock market is often taken as an indicator of the general state of the economy. Still, it is possible for the two to become disconnected. The stock market can be in relatively good shape, but the broader, more general economy is in a recession.

There are many reasons why there is this disconnect. One of the major ones is that the stock market is not by itself a representative of everyone who participates in the actual economy. Stock markets are disproportionately composed of relatively high net worth individuals and large companies that have access to large amounts of investment capital.

Emotional investing and panic can also cause stock movements that are not accompanied by any real changes in the productive activity of the economy. One way you can think of this disconnect is that the economy is the objective reality, and the stock market is the subjective interpretation of the economy. Investors can have an inaccurate subjective interpretation of the actual state of the economy.

5 ECONOMIC FACTORS THAT AFFECT THE STOCK MARKET

Interest Rates

Interest is the main mechanism by which lending institutions make money. They lend out a sum of money and expect it to be paid back in regular installments with interest. You can think of interest rates as the cost that you pay to use someone else's money. In short, when interest rates rise, it makes it harder to borrow money, which means that there is less economic and investing activity. That is why when stock prices are falling and there is little market activity, the Federal Reserve will cut interest rates to stimulate economic activity.

In the US, interest rates and the general money supply are controlled by the Federal Reserve and the Federal Open Market Committee. Both organizations were created with the goal of passing policies that are conducive to the economic growth and well-being of Americans. The Federal Reserve, sometimes called The Fed, was put into place in the early 20th century to stabilize the economy by introducing a centralized monetary policy-making body. The US was inspired to create the Federal Reserve Act after seeing the positive economic effects that banking centralization had on the pre-war economy in Europe.

As such, the Federal Reserve has the authority to determine the country's money supply and set the interest rates that commercial banks use to borrow money from one another. According to the fractional reserve theory of money creation, money is created by banks lending out existing funds. Having low interest rates is, therefore, a necessary condition of a healthy economy as it ensures that banks can keep lending money.

Investors often talk a lot about interest rates, and for a good reason. They play a direct role in how much money is borrowed and how much economic activity there is. If interest rates are too high, then that means that banks have to pay more interest to borrow money, so they are less able to lend money to individuals and businesses. The result is that consumers have less money to spend on things like cars or houses, and businesses cannot afford large-scale capital improvements because of the high cost of borrowing money. The end result is that there is less investment activity because the economy is not producing as much.

More specifically, interest rates in the country are tied to the federal funds rate, which is the rate that banks lend money to one another. The federal fund rate is directly maintained by the Fed and changes daily. It is the standard against which all other interest rates in the country are set, so it's used as an indicator of whether interest rates are falling or rising.

On the flip side, maintaining interest rates is necessary for inflation and to increase the money supply in the country. The problem is that too much inflation can lead to a loss in purchasing power because the value of each individual dollar is more diminutive. Hence, the Fed watches inflation rates through metrics like the Consumer Price index (CPI) and Producer Price Index (PPI) and will raise the federal funds rate to control inflation. However, in times of economic crisis, slashing the federal funds rate can provide a much-needed boost to the economy.

Inflation

Inflation, in essence, is the rise in prices and services over time. On the one hand, inflation is a necessary part of a growing economy. As the available supply of money grows, we would naturally expect this to exert upward pressure on prices. Some inflation is a necessary part of a healthy, growing economy.

However, too much inflation can have negative economic impacts. The main negative effect of inflation is that it decreases the purchasing power of money. If inflation increases after a certain point, it discourages people from buying because prices are too high. The result is that there is less business activity and thus less investment activity. Inflation also has the negative effect of causing saved money to depreciate in value as time goes on.

Inflation can be caused by several things, most often due to increased production costs. As the price of production rises, the price of consumer goods will rise in tandem. The demand for goods has stayed the same, but the supply has decreased due to the increased cost of production. The result is that there is less economic activity because consumers do not have as much disposable income. This translates into decreased stock market performance as investor confidence in the economy stalls.

Inflation can also be caused by increased push or demand for goods and services. When the economy is in good shape, there is a lot of consumer confidence and spending. This increased demand exerts upward pressure on prices. However, as the demand for some goods increases, the supply decreases. The result is that prices can be pushed higher as consumers are willing to pay more. This kind of mechanism is seen in housing markets all the time. Demand for houses drives up the price of houses, but if the supply of homes is too low or does not increase in pace with this increase in demand, then prices will get too high for consumers to reasonably afford. The result is that there is less investment in real estate because the return on investment is less likely.

One of the major ways of measuring inflation is the Consumer Price Index (CPI), which is a measure of the average price of a basket of standard goods and services. Standard goods and services here include food, cars, clothing, education, recreation, etc.

Inflation is not always bad for investments. If you hold shares in an industry in which inflation is causing rising prices, you could stand to profit. For instance, energy stocks would likely go up if the price of energy rose.

So inflation is a double edge sword. It is a natural part of a growing economy, but it cannot outpace increases in productivity. Inflation without an increase in productivity can lead to soaring prices and low investment opportunities.

GDP

GDP stands for Gross Domestic Product and is a measure of the total economic output of a specific entity. Typically, GDP refers to the total economic output of the entire country. GDP is often used as a shorthand indicator of the health of the economy as positive changes in GDP reflect economic growth. GDP can be calculated in many ways but includes private investment wealth, government spending, and exports to foreign countries.

GDP is essential for the stock market as it affects investor sentiment and confidence. Generally, suppose investors see rising GDP numbers. In that case, they take it as a sign that the economy is doing well, and they are incentivized to invest. This change in investing ends up working to increase

GDP by improving the production of goods and services.

Bull markets have an effect on GDP. When equity prices are rising and buying behavior is high, there is a good deal of optimism about the economy. As a result, companies are more likely to issue shares to build up capital for growth and expansion. These actions increase GDP. As you can see, GDP and the stock market share a somewhat cyclical relationship where positive changes in one drive positive changes in the other.

On the other hand, when GDP is falling, investor confidence is low, so there is less investment and consequently less economic activity. In fact, an economic recession is precisely defined as two consecutive quarters of negative GDP growth or contraction. Economic recessions have a feedback effect as negative investor sentiment results in less investment, less economic activity, and less production overall.

Unemployment

Unemployment and the stock market share a fairly direct connection. The US is a consumer-based economy, meaning that the main economic driver is the purchase and consumption of products. High demand for products and services drives the creation of those products and increased economic productivity. Also, most consumers in this country rely on a job as their sole form of income. Thus, when unemployment is high, more people are not receiving an income, so there is less demand for products because people cannot buy things.

The result is that stock prices can drastically fall in areas that are primarily driven by consumer spending. For example, it's well known that when people have less money, they spend less on luxury goods and items. When people are just trying to survive, they don't have enough money to spend on clothes and cars. As buying decreases, this can have a ripple effect across the entire economy and cause the value of the dollar to decrease.

So you might think that when unemployment is low, that must be good for the economy. People have money, and they can buy stuff, right? Like most things with investing, it's not that simple.

When unemployment is very low, many new jobs added to the economy create diminishing returns in value. The value that these jobs produce is not enough to cover the cost of labor. This inefficiency in the utilization of labor markets is known in economic circles as an *output gap* or "slack." Very low unemployment can also lead to wage inflation as companies have to offer more in wages as fewer people are looking for jobs. Interestingly enough, the best historical returns have come after periods of high unemployment.

Additionally, very low unemployment rates can also lead to problems if the Fed changes policy to make new jobs. As such, unemployment is an important aspect of maintaining the balance of the economy. Part of our current model of economic growth relies on there being a pool of unemployed people who can drive demand for jobs and compete for wages, two things that are vital to a growing economy.

Trade Wars

So far, we have only talked about factors that are domestic in nature. However, given that a sizable chunk of the US's economy is based on exports and imports, disruptions of foreign trade can have a serious effect on the economy.

A trade war occurs when one country places high tariffs or restrictions on imports from another country. One motivation for restricting foreign imports is that domestic workers might feel that cheap foreign goods are hurting the domestic economy. Trade wars are often a consequence of this kind of nationalist protectionism, which is antithetical to the general ethos of free trade that has been cultivated among western countries in the past 100 or so years.

Trade wars can also be motivated by what is called a "trade deficit." A trade deficit occurs if a country's imports outweigh its exports. Often, countries will react to a trade deficit by placing restrictions on foreign imports to boost the activity of domestic buying and exports. Trade wars are distinct from sanctions as they are motivated by economic concerns, not necessarily concerns of philanthropy or ethics.

Trade wars are very controversial among economists and investors. Critics of economic policies that favor domestic industries and penalize foreign industries say that they ultimately end up hurting businesses and consumers of both countries because it shuts off opportunities for increased growth, cooperation, and cultural exchange. Critics also claim that trade wars can hurt domestic populations because it limits the selection of consumer goods they have access to.

Trade wars can also negatively affect businesses that rely on foreign imports for operations. For example, if domestic companies have to pay more for raw materials from foreign companies, it could decrease overall productivity and rising prices rather than incentivizing domestic businesses to buy from domestic sources. This is especially true for industries that may rely on imported material and resources that are hard to come by in the country.

However, proponents of protectionist economic policies say that they provide stability and protection to domestic interests. Specifically, trade unions might petition for increased tariffs to protect their industry from being undercut by cheap foreign labor and products. Proponents also claim that economic protectionism increases domestic development opportunities and promotes local job growth.

As a recent example of a trade war in the media, during his 2016 presidential campaign, President Donald Trump promised to enact protectionist policies to protect American manufacturing jobs from being outsourced to foreign nations such as India and China. Trump also threatened to pull the US out of the World Trade Organization. In 2018, in retaliation to threats over IP fines, the Chinese government instituted a 25% tax on all US imports.

As far as the stock market goes, trade wars can have a negative effect. The economic uncertainty that they bring can cause low investor confidence, which results in decreased investment activity.

FINAL WORDS

The economy and stock market are not synonymous and should not be treated as such. While they do share a tight relationship, they are conceptually and practically distinct. The stock market is often used as an indicator of the general state of the economy. Moreover, factors in the general economy can have an effect on the stock market and vice versa.

In many ways, the two share a cyclical relationship. Changes in the economy affect investor behavior, which in turn affects economic activity and productivity, which in turn affects the economy, and so on and so forth. The back and forth dynamic is why economic crises can quickly spiral out of control as poor investor sentiment inevitably pulls down economic performance, and poor economic performance pulls down investor sentiment.

3 INSIDER SECRETS TO THE MARKET

We have covered the basics of stocks, different types of investments, methods of stock analysis and evaluation, and how the broader economy affects the activity of the stock market. But pure theoretical knowledge will only take you so far. Like any kind of endeavor, investing is a practice and skill you must cultivate. Do you ever wonder how people like Warren Buffett have the uncanny ability to make excellent investment decisions and predictions? It's because they are experts and have spent decades fine-tuning their investment sense.

It's the same principle behind practicing a sport. Once you get really good at your golf swing, the process becomes second nature and intuitive. Expert investors can "see" good investments as they have trained their faculties to recognize subtle features. Over time, you can cultivate this skill and hone your investment "sixth sense."

But in the meantime, that doesn't mean there aren't tips and tricks you can use to help get the upper hand in the stock market. When it comes to stocks, *information* is key. Investors will sleep on some huge tip they got and not tell anyone else. After all, if everyone were privy to that knowledge, then it would effectively be worthless. This is one major reason why the biggest investors try very hard to keep their actual investments secret. The more people know about potential winning investments, the less lucrative they can become.

So if you really want to gain from the market, you need to be careful with the information you get and find the right kind of insider info. Luckily for you, we have a ton of great sources where you can get this kind of insider info.

OPEN INSIDER

Open Insider is a great resource if you want to find stocks that are being bought with some insider knowledge. Open Insider is an open-source resource that tracks transactions on the stock market. Basically, Open Insider can tell you who is trading, when they are doing it, and how much they are trading for.

In other words, Open Insider is a source where you can track potential insider trading. **Insider trading** refers to the trading of a company's stock by someone who is using non-public material information about that stock. Depending on when the transaction takes place, insider trading can be legal or illegal. Insider trading is technically illegal when the information used is material to stock performance and not publicly available. However, that doesn't mean that institutions often find loopholes and technicalities to get around these rules.

Open Insider is great as it provides a source of potential insider trading information. You can search for transactions based on the stock being traded, when the stock was traded, how many shares changed hands, and who was doing the trading.

The last point is probably the most important. Open Insider lets you search for transactions in trades by CEOs, CFOs, CTOs, and other officer titles of companies. Since these people are often closest to pertinent material information about stocks, these kinds of people's stock movements can hint that something is about to happen. For example, suppose you see the CEO of a company dumping a ton of their shares. In that case, that could be a sign that the company will go through some hardship in the near future.

Here is what I have found works best for Open Insider. Ensure that you are searching for cluster buys of large volumes, specifically by directors in the company (CEO, CFO, CTO, etc.). You can also eliminate any buys or sales less than $150,000 as these likely won't matter to you. With these parameters, you are much more likely to identify good candidates to buy by following insider behavior.

As a real-world example of this kind of insider trading, back in November 2020, the CEO of Pfizer Pharmaceuticals, Albert Bourla, dumped 62% of his stock right after an announcement about the success of their COVID-19 vaccine shortly after shares had jumped by 7% following the announcement. Apparently, this trade was the first public trade that Bourla made since 2016. Many believe that Bourla scheduled the trade after learning about the successful trial results before they went public.

So, following insider trading from parties that are in the know can be a way to follow along with stock movements. Since insiders often have superior information, they can better predict future stock movements. According to some sources, insider traders are able to beat the average market return by nearly 6%. The key thing is to look for when large institutions or officials *buy* large quantities of stock. Insiders will sell stock for a ton of different reasons, but they typically only buy stock for one reason: they think the share price is going to rise.

So, if you want to make sure that you are working with the most up-to-date information, then you should definitely check out Open Insider. It is 100% free to use, does not require any sign up or registration; who knows, maybe Open Insider will help you find a hidden trading opportunity to make. You can find it at http://openinsider.com.

SENATE STOCK WATCHER

Suppose you are looking for another good source to identify insider trading strategies. In that case, Senate Stock Watcher is another good source to use. Senate Stock Watcher keeps tabs on all of our elected officials and what kinds of stock transactions they make. As much as we would like to think otherwise, politicians often have an agenda. They will use their knowledge of governmental policy and insider secrets to make trades. For example, elected officials have a history of selling off lots of stock before new legislation that might hurt a sector is announced, or they might buy shares when impending legislation will be good for their portfolios.

Given that senators are required to report recent stock transactions, Senate Stock Watcher is an open-source, free resource for keeping tabs on elected officials' trading activity. The website says that it is for purely non-partisan reasons and is meant to increase governmental transparency. However, the savvy investor can definitely use this information to their advantage. Suppose they notice a large number of officials buying or selling specific shares. In that case, that could be a sign that some legislation or policy might affect the economy and stock market.

So, Senate Stock Watcher is not only a good resource for the responsible citizen concerned with transparency but can also be a useful resource for investors looking for a hot tip. The US has a law called the Stop Trading on Congressional Knowledge (STOCK) Act that explicitly prohibits Congress and senators from making trades based on official information that is not public yet.

This kind of insider trading from our elected officials is probably more commonplace than most would be comfortable to admit. For example, there was a huge scandal back in early 2020 in which several elected officials were accused of abusing non-public knowledge about COVID-19 to sell off assets and avoid the massive stock market crash that happened in March 2020. However, no one brought any formal charges against anyone. In fact, Senate Stock Watcher was created just a month after this supposed scandal to make sure there is transparency among our elected officials.

However, you are not an elected official, so why shouldn't you be able to use their movements to glean information? If they are going to use their special knowledge to take advantage, you should also be able to. There is also a companion website called Congress Stock watcher that keeps tabs on stock transactions from House of Representatives members.

You can find these at www.senatestockwatcher.com and www. housestockwatcher.com.

The Securities and Exchange Commission (SEC) is a governmental body that seeks to protect investors and promote fairness in markets by passing trading regulations. The SEC website is also a resource for figuring out insider secrets for all institutions and investment managers. The SEC requires all trading institutions and investment managers that manage over $100 million in assets must disclose all equity holdings. These equity holdings can give you a good idea of what kinds of buys the largest and richest corporations and investment institutions are doing.

So, if you want to find this info, here is how you do it. Go to SEC.gov and click on the tab near the top labeled **Filing**. Click on this tab, then scroll down to the tab labeled "EDGAR-Search and Access," and click on EDGAR full-text search. This search function will let you look at all relevant information about filings from large institutions.

Once there, type in the words "Form 13F" and hit search. You can then browse all Form 13F forms from large institutions. Form 13F is required by the SEC and provides info on equity allocations from these large firms. In other words, by looking for these forms, you can see what the largest institutions are buying and selling. These equity allocations can give you hints on what stocks might be a good buy right now. Form 13F provides transparency to the public and shows what the top institutional investors and market makers are doing right now.

The SEC website also has pretty much any official document on trading bodies that you need. You can find new filings of companies, rules surrounding legislation and regulation, pending litigation, press releases, and public statements. You can find pretty much any pertinent information you need there.

OTHER TIPS TO FIND INSIDER SECRETS

I have given you some of my favorite sources to find insider secrets and get special knowledge, but there are plenty of other sources to check out. Here are a few tips to keep in mind when you are trolling around for stock secrets and insider information.

- **General Counsel and Lawyers.** Most companies have a "general" or "senior" counsel who is that company's top lawyer. Lawyers tend to be highly risk-averse, especially with their large corporate clients. So, they typically are cautious about buying stocks. So, if you see a general counsel or senior counsel for a company buying a lot of shares, that could be a strong signal that something good is about to happen. Like we said earlier, insiders might sell shares for several reasons. But they only buy them for one: they think that it will make money.
- **Look for large "cluster" trades.** One thing to look out for is large volume trades from institutional insiders. These large bodies might make smaller trades all the time, but those small trades are rarely an indicator of anything big. Large volume trades, especially ones made by institutional traders, are a sign that something big is about to go down. If groups of insiders are buying all at the same time, then it is a powerful signal that they are working with some kind of privileged knowledge.
- **Look for infrequent buys.** A good chunk of institutional buyers buy and sell shares multiple times during the year. However, many make very few trades throughout the year. If you notice that an entity that normally does not make many transactions is suddenly buying a lot of shares, then some juicy information might have spurred them out of their trading doldrums. Insiders that rarely ever buy shares but are now doing it a lot are a strong signal that it's a good time to jump into trading.

FINAL WORDS

Insider trading is commonly seen as a negative thing as it gives some people an unfair advantage when it comes to buying and selling. However, there are several ways that you can identify potential cases of insider trading and benefit from following what those in the know are doing. If someone who has special information is making a lot of buys, there is a good reason why they are doing so. They think that those buys will make them a lot of money.

So, you can use these resources to get a leg up on the competition. The major resources I shared in this chapter are 100% free to use and do not require you to make an account or anything like that. Once you get used to combing through the data, it becomes pretty easy to see when there is some kind of insider trading going on.

MAKING MONEY WHILE SLEEPING

We are nearing the close of our journey, and hopefully, you have learned a lot. You should be able to analyze stocks and make solid picks using the information and methods of analysis that we have covered. You now even know how to find insider information to have better chances of making a profit.

One of the most critical parts of successful investing is figuring out ways to maximize your returns. Every moment that your money is not working for you is future potential income lost. As such, you need to set things up with your investments so you can continually make money, even when you are sleeping.

PASSIVE INCOME

We have talked about this already, but we want to take this chapter to talk about making passive income more. Passive income is just that, income that you get that you do not have to work for. For many, passive income is thought to be the Holy Grail of investing. "You mean I can make money from not doing anything??" It might sound like a free lunch that is too good to be true, but many successful investors manage to live off their passive income so they never have to worry about work again.

Passive income, in a nutshell, is money that you make in the background. As such, you can set up your investments to generate passive income when you are not actively trying to make money.

How might you ask? There are a ton of ways. Let's look at just a few of the more popular options.

INVESTING FOR DIVIDENDS

As a recap, dividends are a portion of company earnings that are doled out to shareholders. Dividends are different from capital gains because they are a direct cash payment to shareholders based on the number of shares that they have. Dividends are a popular option for peoples' retirement because they can provide a steady income stream while you are not working.

So how do you go about investing for dividends?

It's simple; you look for stocks that have a high dividend yield. Remember, the dividend yield is equal to the ratio of the total amount of dividends produced by a share divided by the share price. So if a share of stock generates $4 per share in dividends and costs $100 per share, then the dividend yield would be ($4/$100) x 100 = **4%.** The goal is to hold enough shares in a company that generates enough dividends to finance your life.

When you are younger and do not need to rely on dividends for your income, you can engage in what is called dividend reinvestment programs. Dividend reinvestment programs allow you to take those dividends and put them right back into your investments. So you get the dividends, and they use those dividends to buy more shares so you can generate more dividends down the road. When you are younger and do not need to rely on dividends for your income, the smartest idea to maximize your returns is to reinvest all your dividends. Fortunately, most online brokers nowadays give you the option to reinvest any dividends that you generate automatically.

When you are nearing retirement, you can start trying to live off those dividends. So, you will need to find safe dividend stocks that can deliver a good dividend yield. The majority of experts agree that 4%-6% are a good, stable dividend yield that companies can sustain for a long time. Several stocks might have a higher dividend yield of 8%-10%. Still, these are often relatively unstable, and it is unlikely they will be able to maintain such high dividend payouts for an extended period. For example, real estate investments tend to have very high dividend yields, but they are often not stable and cannot maintain that high rate for very long.

With that in mind, here is a selection of some of the best dividend stocks you can get your hands on right now.

Microsoft (NASDAQ: MSFT)

Microsoft has long been a stable dividend stock in addition to being one of the largest companies by market capitalization in the world. Microsoft's quarterly results are always excellent in terms of revenue. The company has managed to increase its dividends annually for almost 15 years and has recently initiated a hike of 9.8%. Their recent heavy investments in cloud infrastructure and AI have put them on the map for one of the best dividend and growth stocks to buy right now.

Coca-Cola (NYSE: KO)

Coca-Cola is one of a handful of companies that have managed to increase dividend payouts every year for over 50 years, and they are showing no signs of slowing down anytime soon. Coca-Cola pays out dividends to investors 4 times per year on April 1, July 1, October 1, and December 15. They also allow you to receive dividend payments either through a direct deposit or via a physical check in the currency of their choice.

Colgate-Palmolive Co. (NYSE: CL)

Colgate-Palmolive is one of the biggest names when it comes to consumer staples and creates all kinds of household use products. From Palmolive soap to Colgate fresh toothpaste, they have their hands in pretty much every aspect of home goods in some capacity. Colgate has managed to produce consistent dividends since 1895 and is currently sitting at a 2.5% dividend yield average over the last 50 years. Colgate-Palmolive is also a giant in one of the most stable industries that there is; consumer staples.

Johnson & Johnson (NYSE: JNJ)

J&J is another huge company with its hands in consumer staples, household goods, and pharmaceutical research. J&J has long been a favorite of dividend investors because they are a huge, stable blue-chip stock and is one of just two blue-chip stocks that have a AAA credit rating, meaning the company has an essentially flawless record when it comes to paying its debts to creditors and shareholders. Johnson & Johnson has been providing dividends since 1963 and is currently standing at a 2.7% year-over-year dividend yield since the '70s.

Black & Decker (NYSE: SWK)

Equipment and tool manufacturer Stanley Black & Decker has been around since the mid-1800s and is one of the oldest companies on the NYSE. Black and Decker have paid out dividends to investors every year since the close of the Civil War and have managed to increase dividend yields for investors every year since. They are currently sitting at a 2.3% dividend yield over the past 50 years.

Church & Dwight (NTSE: CHD)

Many people have never heard of Church & Dwight, but they most certainly have heard of and used their products before. Church and Dwight is the entity that owns Arm & Hammer, one of their most well-known brands and product lines. Aside from household cleaning products, C&D is behind some of the most well-known household good brand names out there, including

OxiClean, Orajel, Trojan, Nair, and more. C&D has a 119-year long dividend history, and their current average dividend yield over the past 50 years is 1.5%.

PPG Industries (NYSE: PPG)

Originally named Pittsburgh Plate Glass, PPG changed its name to PPG Industries in the late 60s and significantly branched out its product catalog from glass. PPG has its hands in a ton of industrial applications and materials like solvents, fiberglass, adhesives, and paints. They have a highly diverse product line of industrial materials which means they always have a good source of income. PPG has been paying out dividends for over 100 years, and they are one of the very few companies that managed to not only survive but actually *increase* dividend payouts during the Great Depression.

General Mills (NYSE: GIS)

Known as the company behind Cheerios, Haagen-Dazs ice cream, and several other popular food brands, General Mills has always been a top contender for best dividend stocks through the years. General Mills has been paying dividends since 1898 and has managed to increase dividend yields for 15 years straight. Since General Mills is in the business of consumer staples, they have a consistent market presence, even during recessions. In fact, General Mills actually saw a nice 15% bump in share prices during the COVID-19 pandemic as more people were buying food products and eating at home rather than dining out.

HOW TO CHOOSE DIVIDEND STOCKS

One of the most important things to look for in dividend stock is companies that have good cash flow and low earnings expectations on average of 5%-10%. Several companies have much higher profit margins and earnings estimates, but they normally cannot keep those numbers up year after year. You want to invest in companies that can manage stable, year-after-year growth. A company might have shown 30% growth in the past year, but it is highly unlikely that they will be able to keep that pace up any longer. So, 5%-10% average growth during the year is a good benchmark. You should be wary of companies that have estimated growth rates of 15% or higher.

You also need to look for stocks from companies that have good cash flow. This is one reason why utility companies and consumer staples tend to be excellent dividends investments. These kinds of companies are relatively recession-proof and make a lot of cash by selling products and services directly to consumers.

You can also look at the historical track record of companies to see how their dividend yields have fared over time. I would highly recommend only considering companies that have managed to generate their current dividend yields for at least the past 5 years. 5 years is a good time frame to determine whether the company is in a good position to stick around and keep producing results.

As far as things to avoid, stay away from companies with some kind of long-term debt on their plate that outweighs their equity. Each company has what is known as a debt-to-equity ratio, which can be calculated by dividing the total amount of a company's liabilities by its shareholder equity. The higher the D/E ratio, the more the company owes to other people, and the less of their earnings they will be able to put into dividends. All other things being equal, we recommend staying away from companies that have a D/E ratio higher than 2.00.

Lastly, it can be very helpful to check industry and sector trends. Looking at macro-level trends is a way that you can get a complete picture of the present and what the future might hold. As a real example, many younger investors are currently investing in healthcare and healthcare services. As the baby boomer population ages, there will likely be a massive spike in demand for medical services. This kind of expected change in the macro-level of the market could be a good sign for future dividend payments from healthcare companies.

One of the best features of dividend stocks is that they can serve as a nice hedge against inflation over the years. As long as your dividend payouts outpace the rate of inflation, reinvesting those funds will ensure that you are always coming out on top and your investments are not losing value.

To sum up, features of the best dividend stocks include high cash flow, low (<10%) but stable projected earnings, and low debt-to-equity ratios. You also want to look for stocks that have historically good dividend yields over a timespan of greater than 5 years.

OTHER TYPES OF INCOME INVESTMENTS

Dividend stocks are one of the best methods of income investments, but there are plenty of other kinds of assets that generate regular income.

Real Estate

For many people, real estate is one of the best methods of income investing. The main reason why this is possible is that real estate and rental properties can generate rent every month, which is a nice consistent flow of cash. In fact, many investors will take out a mortgage to buy a property, then rent it out to pay off that mortgage. This rental income can also serve as a source of passive income in old age. Investing in real estate is a great idea because you can generate a consistent stream of rental income, but also because the property market is relatively consistent and tends to appreciate in value over time.

In fact, many investors might consider real estate to be the ultimate long-term investment. Real estate is not very liquid as it can be hard to sell once you get your hands on it. But historically, real estate has been a very stable market and has managed to hit an average market return of 6% over the past 100 years. Believe it or not, some of the wealthiest people in history have made their fortunes through real estate investing.

Bonds

Bonds are another type of investment for income and a good choice at that. A bond is a loan that you issue to some entity, with the promise of being paid back plus interest by a certain date. Bonds are considered a fixed-income asset as they generate fixed interest payments every period.

There are many different types of bonds with different interest rates, maturation dates, and holders. The two most common types are corporate bonds and US treasury bonds. Corporate bonds are issued by large corporations and serve the same purpose as shares: they are a way of raising capital funding for projects and expansion. The main difference is that bonds do not give the holder any kinds of ownership or voting rights.

The other kind of bond is US treasury bonds. These are issued by the government and generate income through fixed-interest payments. Many investors consider US treasury bonds to be the most stable kind of investment on the planet because they are backed by the full faith and credit of the US government, one of the most powerful institutions in the world. The only way a treasury bond would fall through is if the US government crumbled, and if that happened, your investment portfolio would probably be the least of your worries.

Bonds are considered low-risk, low-return investments, but they are comparatively stable compared to stocks. Stocks have managed an average 10% return over the past 100 years and bonds around 6%. That is definitely less, but the lower returns are made up for by how stable and reliable bond payments are.

You can buy bonds individually, and they are also a major component of many index funds and ETFs. For example, the iShare Core US Aggregate Bond ETF (NYSEARCA: AGG) holds a spread of over 8,000 corporate and government bonds.

Annuities

Annuities are another old investment vehicle, but they have been picking up in popularity in the past few years. Annuities are essentially fixed-income investments that pay you a monthly lump sum payment through your retirements. Annuities can be a good way to ensure that you have a steady stream of income that will not be affected by changing dividend yields.

With an annuity, you slowly put money into it over the years, and it grows in value through investments. Then, when retirement hits, you can start to receive regular income payments from that annuity. In other words, it's almost like giving yourself an allowance for retirement.

The main catch is that you have to pay into annuities for several years before you can start getting distributions. In that sense, annuities function a lot like life insurance in that they only start paying out benefits after a long time. Annuities also often have very strict limitations on their uses, so if you are thinking about paying into one, make sure that you read all the fine print of any annuity agreement you are signing.

AVOID FEAR AND GREED

A common saying is that there are two primary forces that drive investor behavior: *fear* and *greed*. This saying is so true that CNNMoney literally created the fear and greed index, which is meant to measure whether a stock is fairly priced. The idea behind this measurement is that fear can make stocks go down from selling and low investor confidence, and greed makes share prices go up as buying increases.

Fear comes in two kinds: fear of losing money and fear of missing out. Pretty much every investor knows what it is like to fear losing your own money with a bad investment. With smart investing and diversification, you can significantly reduce the fear of losing money.

However, the other kind of fear, fear of missing out (or FOMO, as it is sometimes called), is much harder to get rid of. People always fear not matching up to the performance of their peers, whether it's because they can't buy that fancy car or they don't make as much in the stock market. FOMO is what makes people make stupid financial decisions, like renting that big apartment because you can "afford" the payment or other expensive luxury items that are not worth the depreciation.

The only way to get out of this crutch is not to care how others are faring. After all, your money is your concern, and no one else needs to know about it. Think of it this way, even if you make fewer gains than your peers, *you would still be better off than you were before*. There is no rational reason to have FOMO, but humans are irrational creatures.

As far as greed goes, greed is maybe not as powerful as fear, but it is important nonetheless. Greed can also be split into two: greed to keep your money and greed to make more money. The former kind of greed is pretty understandable. After all, you worked hard for your money; why wouldn't you want to keep it? The second kind of greed is what can get you in trouble in the stock market. The desire to make more and more money can make you take dumb risks for diminishing returns.

A lot of investors will completely ignore obvious bad signs because they are enticed by the prospect of "easy money." That is one reason why the dot-com bubble burst of 2000 was so bad. Everyone could see the signs that the bubble was about to pop, but every investor figured *they* were smart enough to get out before share prices tanked. Unfortunately, *someone* had to lose, and for a very large portion of investors, they were on the losing end of their bets.

That is why many investors say you need to take the emotion out of the practice. Very often, things like fear and greed can cloud your judgment. So if you are a highly emotional investor, then you need ways to avoid those kinds of influences.

Ultimately, the thing that should drive you to invest is a careful analysis of your goals. If you are investing primarily to set yourself up for retirement, then you want to make sure that you have a clear vision of what that endpoint looks like and how you can get there. This is where something like a financial advisor can come in handy. These professionals can help you sort out a suitable plan for your future and help make a roadmap to get there.

11

CONCLUSIONS

If you have made it all the way here, congratulations! 30,000 words later, and you are still with us! We know it has been a long journey, so hopefully, you have learned a lot. If you are keeping track at home, you have learned about

- Markets
- What stock markets are
- How stock markets work
- Features of stocks
- Different metrics for gauging stocks
- The different types of changes and why they are important
- Tools to navigate exchanges
- How to manage sectors and industries
- The difference between mutual funds and ETFs
- The basics of technical and fundamental analysis
- Trading strategies for beginners
- How the economy and stock market are related
- How to take advantage of insider secrets
- How to set up passive income for life
- And more

These topics will serve you well for the rest of your life while you are navigating the waters of the stock market. You should be able to make an investment account, find good investment picks, and manage risk in line with your investment preferences and goals.

One last piece of advice I have for all you new investors who are no doubt chomping at the bit to get out there and start trading: Don't be so preoccupied with what your peers are doing and how they are trading. People like to act like there is a "right" way to invest and that any other way is somehow deficient. The bottom line is that the "right" way to invest is whatever way helps you meet your financial and life goals. If that involves day-trading to scalp as many profits as you can or solely focusing on long-term investments for retirement, then that is the "right" way to invest for you.

To be clear, there is nothing wrong with taking advice from your peers or even studying their trading strategies to see how successful they are. Rather, you should not use their investment goals as your own. Some people will have a higher risk tolerance than you, and others will want to make larger short-term returns. What matters is that you find a strategy that works for you and stick to it.

There is also never a better time to get started investing than the present. So don't be discouraged if you do not have a complete and detailed plan laid out at the beginning. A lot of investors don't figure out a trading strategy that works for them until they experiment a bit. Of course, this means you definitely will see some losses, but that is an inevitable occurrence. Your best bet at the beginning is to start small and then work your way to more extensive, riskier investments.

In fact, if you wait too long, you are ultimately hurting your future income potential. Think about it: imagine you invested $100,000 over 10 years with an average return of 8%, you would have about $215,892. However, what if you had started 5 years earlier and invested for 15 years? Then you would have around $317,216, over 30% more. Keep in mind that these numbers assume that you don't add anything else to your investment principle over time, so the actual numbers will likely be higher. The only time better than today to invest is yesterday. Since you don't have a time machine (or at least, I'm assuming you don't), your best bet is to start today.

At the beginning of this book, I said that we are in the middle of a financial revolution. The means and methods of investing are now widely available to everyone so that you can play on terms with the big stock market players.

The days of letting the big, rich, institutional traders have all the fun are over, and the time of the average everyday investor is here.

As these barriers to entry have been broken down, more people are taking their financial future into their own hands. What's more, they are succeeding in doing it. The new world has shown that you don't have to grind out that boring 9-5 job just to be rewarded with pitiful wages that won't keep up with inflation. You can make your fortune, all on your own, through investing.

For many, the prospect of financial independence equals freedom. And let's be honest, who doesn't want to be free from the stresses and everyday worries of money? Through investing, you can achieve peace of mind and have the freedom to focus on the things in life that you really care about. And frankly, that is the entire point of investing in the first place.

If you enjoyed this book, please leave a review on Amazon!